I0436515

Disclaimer:

The information in this book is designed to provide accurate and actionable information regarding the subject matter. This book is written and sold with the understanding that the publisher and author is not engaged in offering compliance, legal, advertising, accounting, compliance, financial, investment or other professional advice.

If you require legal, financial, account, marketing, compliance, or other professional services, consult your compliance department, services of a professional, etc.

The author and publisher of this book are not financial advisors and do not hold any professional investment licenses. The information presented in this book is based on data available at the time of writing and should not be interpreted as an endorsement of any cryptocurrency, company, ETF, or specific investment strategy.

Investments in cryptocurrency ETFs and other financial instruments carry inherent risks, and the performance of these instruments can be highly volatile. It is recommended that readers conduct their own research, consider their personal financial circumstances, and consult with a qualified financial professional before making any investment decisions.

The author and publisher of this book shall not be held liable for any direct, indirect, incidental, consequential, or punitive damages arising out of access to, use of, or reliance on any content in this book, including, but not limited to, any errors or omissions in any content, or any loss or damage of any kind incurred as a result of the use of any content posted, transmitted, or otherwise made available via this book.

By reading this book, you agree to indemnify and hold harmless the author and publisher from any claim, demand, action, damage, loss, or expense of any kind, relating to or arising from the content of this book.

About the Author:

Andy LaPointe spent 15 years in the corporate world as a Registered Investment Advisor (RIA) and mutual fund/separate account wholesaler. He is the author of several crypto education books and courses. He is a corporate advisor and equity investor in a digital asset start-up.

Please contact us for special quantity discounts and special promotions to use for sales promotions, educational and training purposes. In addition, Mr. LaPointe is available for keynote speeches, sales training, consulting and more.

For more information contact CryptoWisdom.com

Check out other titles in the Crypto Wisdom Series:

- *Crypto Wisdom: An Investor's Comprehensive Guide to Digital Asset Research and Analysis: A Step-by-Step Guide to Researching and Analyzing Digital Assets for Building Winning Portfolios*

- *Crypto Wisdom: An Investor's Comprehensive Guide to Digital Asset Portfolio Management: A Step-by-Step Guide for Building Winning Crypto Portfolios*

- *The Financial Advisor's Digital Asset Practice Guide: A Step-by-Step Guide to Building a Digital Asset Practice*

- *The Investment Advisor's Cryptocurrency Roadmap: The Guide to Offering Cryptocurrencies and Digital Assets in Your Practice*

- *Mastering the Crypto ETF Wave: A Comprehensive Guide to Researching and Investing*

Visit **www.CryptoWisdom.com** for complete step-by-step training, cryptocurrency educational videos, etc.

Contents

Introduction to "Crypto ETFs in the Financial Advisor's Toolkit: Enhancing Client Wealth"

Welcome to "Crypto ETFs in the Financial Advisor's Toolkit: Enhancing Client Wealth," a comprehensive and insightful exploration into the burgeoning world of cryptocurrency Exchange-Traded Funds (ETFs). This book is crafted to be an indispensable resource for financial advisors, investment professionals, and anyone intrigued by the integration of traditional financial advising with the rapidly evolving landscape of digital assets.

As the financial world witnesses an unprecedented era of innovation, cryptocurrencies have emerged not just as a novel asset class but also as a catalyst for change in investment strategies. This evolution has given birth to crypto ETFs, blending the familiarity and regulatory framework of traditional ETFs with the dynamic, high-growth potential of cryptocurrencies.

In this book, we delve into the multifaceted aspects of crypto ETFs and how they can be effectively incorporated into modern financial advisory practices. Aimed at enhancing client wealth and diversifying investment portfolios, the chapters unfold a comprehensive understanding of crypto ETFs, their mechanics, market implications, and potential impact on wealth management.

We begin by laying the foundational knowledge of cryptocurrencies and ETFs, followed by an in-depth analysis of how these two worlds converge in crypto ETFs. This book also navigates through the complex regulatory landscape, offering insights into how it shapes the market and investment opportunities.

For financial advisors seeking to refine their practice, the book offers strategies for assessing client profiles, understanding risk tolerance, and tailoring advice to include crypto ETFs in investment portfolios. We also explore the significance of staying abreast of technological advancements and adapting to the changing financial landscape to better serve clients in this new era.

The latter part of the book is dedicated to future-forward thinking, discussing emerging trends, potential new products, and services in the crypto ETF space. It provides advisors with foresight into how they can evolve their practices to not only stay relevant but also to capitalize on new opportunities.

"Crypto ETFs in the Financial Advisor's Toolkit: Enhancing Client Wealth" is more than just a guide; it's a pathway to understanding and leveraging one of the most significant financial innovations of our time. It equips financial advisors with the knowledge, tools, and confidence to navigate the complex yet rewarding world of crypto ETFs, ultimately enhancing their ability to guide clients towards sustainable wealth creation in the digital age.

Overview of Cryptocurrency and ETFs

In the realm of modern finance, two distinct but increasingly interconnected concepts have risen to prominence: cryptocurrencies and Exchange-Traded Funds (ETFs). This chapter provides an overview of these innovative financial instruments, laying the groundwork for understanding their convergence in the form of crypto ETFs.

Cryptocurrencies, at their core, are digital or virtual currencies that use cryptography for security. The most defining feature of these digital assets is their decentralized nature, typically operating on blockchain technology — a distributed ledger that records all transactions across a network of computers. Bitcoin, introduced in 2009, was the first cryptocurrency, and since then, thousands of others, like Ethereum and Ripple, have emerged. These digital assets are known for their volatility, but they also offer possibilities for high returns, attracting a wide range of investors.

Exchange-Traded Funds (ETFs), on the other hand, are marketable securities that track an index, commodity, bonds, or a basket of assets like an index fund. Unlike mutual funds, which only trade once a day after the market closes, ETFs trade throughout the day on stock exchanges. Their appeal lies in their lower expense ratios and tax efficiency compared to mutual funds.

The integration of these two concepts has led to the development of cryptocurrency ETFs. Crypto ETFs aim to provide investors with exposure to the cryptocurrency market without the complexities of directly buying, holding, and managing these digital assets. They offer a regulated, more familiar investment structure, making them an appealing option for a broader range of investors looking to tap into the potential of cryptocurrencies.

As we delve deeper into subsequent chapters, we'll explore the intricacies, benefits, and challenges of crypto ETFs, and how they're transforming the landscape of investment options.

Definition of Cryptocurrencies and ETFs

In the rapidly evolving world of finance, two terms have garnered significant attention: cryptocurrencies and Exchange-Traded Funds (ETFs). This chapter delves into the fundamental aspects of these financial instruments, elucidating their core principles, mechanisms, and the innovative ways they are transforming the investment landscape.

Cryptocurrencies: A Digital Revolution in Currency

Cryptocurrencies represent a paradigm shift in the concept of money. They are digital or virtual currencies that use cryptography for security, making them nearly impossible to counterfeit. The most defining feature of cryptocurrencies is their decentralized nature, typically operating on a technology called blockchain—a distributed ledger enforced by a disparate network of computers. This decentralization stands in stark contrast to traditional, centralized financial systems and fiat currencies controlled by governments and central banks.

The inception of cryptocurrencies can be traced back to 2009 with the launch of Bitcoin, the first and most well-known cryptocurrency. Since then, the cryptocurrency market has expanded rapidly, encompassing thousands of unique cryptocurrencies serving various purposes. These digital assets are characterized by their volatility, high liquidity, and the potential for significant returns, which attract both retail and institutional investors.

ETFs: Simplifying Investment in Diverse Assets

Exchange-Traded Funds (ETFs) are a more recent innovation in the world of finance, gaining popularity for their simplicity and efficiency. An ETF is a type of security that tracks an index, commodity, sector, or other assets, but can be bought and sold on a stock exchange the same way a regular stock can. A key attribute of ETFs is their ability to offer diversified exposure to a wide range of investments, including stocks, bonds, commodities, and now, increasingly, cryptocurrencies.

ETFs offer several advantages over traditional mutual funds. They typically have lower expense ratios and are more tax-efficient. Moreover, the ability to trade ETFs on stock exchanges means they offer greater liquidity and flexibility, allowing investors to react swiftly to market changes during trading hours.

Crypto ETFs: Bridging Traditional and Digital Finance

Crypto ETFs represent an intersection of these two revolutionary financial products. They provide a way for investors to gain exposure to the cryptocurrency market without the complexities of directly buying, holding, and securing these digital assets. This is particularly appealing to traditional investors who are accustomed to the regulated environment of stock exchanges but are intrigued by the potential of cryptocurrencies.

There are two main types of crypto ETFs: physical-backed and synthetic. Physical-backed crypto ETFs hold actual cryptocurrencies in their portfolio, whereas synthetic ones use derivatives to track the performance of digital currencies. Each type offers different risk profiles and exposure levels to the cryptocurrency market, catering to a diverse range of investment strategies and risk appetites.

Conclusion

The convergence of cryptocurrencies and ETFs symbolizes a significant shift in modern investment strategies. Cryptocurrencies, with their decentralized, digital nature, represent a new frontier in finance, while ETFs provide a familiar, regulated framework for investment. Together, they offer innovative avenues for portfolio diversification and wealth growth, making them crucial components in the toolkit of contemporary investors and financial advisors. As the financial landscape continues to evolve, understanding these instruments becomes essential for navigating the dynamic world of investment.

Historical Context and Evolution

This chapter provides an insightful journey through the historical context and evolution of cryptocurrencies and Exchange-Traded Funds (ETFs), tracing their origins and the transformative impact they have had on the financial world.

The Emergence and Growth of Exchange-Traded Funds (ETFs)

The history of ETFs began in the early 1990s, marking a significant innovation in the world of investment funds. The first successful ETF in the United States, the Standard & Poor's Depositary Receipts (SPDR), was launched in 1993. This fund, commonly known as the "Spider", tracked the S&P 500 index and allowed investors to trade index portfolios just like stocks. The appeal of ETFs quickly caught on due to their low cost, tax efficiency, and ease of trading, leading to a diverse range of ETFs covering various asset classes, including stocks, bonds, commodities, and real estate.

Over the years, ETFs have evolved, with the introduction of innovative products like inverse ETFs, which move in the opposite direction of their underlying index, and leveraged ETFs, which use financial derivatives to amplify returns. This evolution reflects the industry's response to investor demand for more sophisticated investment tools and strategies.

The Advent and Rise of Cryptocurrencies

Cryptocurrencies emerged as a radical innovation in digital technology. The genesis of cryptocurrencies can be traced back to 2008 when an individual (or group) under the pseudonym Satoshi Nakamoto published a whitepaper titled "Bitcoin: A Peer-to-Peer Electronic Cash System". This whitepaper laid the foundation for Bitcoin, the world's first cryptocurrency, which was launched in January 2009. Bitcoin introduced the concept of a decentralized digital currency, operating on a blockchain technology framework, which ensured security, transparency, and immutability of transactions.

The success of Bitcoin paved the way for the development of thousands of other cryptocurrencies, each with unique functionalities and underlying technologies. Notable among these are Ethereum, Ripple, and Litecoin, each contributing to the expanding ecosystem of digital currencies. The cryptocurrency market has witnessed exponential growth, characterized by high volatility and speculative investment, drawing attention from both retail and institutional investors.

Intersection of ETFs and Cryptocurrencies

The intersection of ETFs and cryptocurrencies represents a significant milestone in financial innovation. As cryptocurrencies gained popularity, there emerged a demand for investment products that could provide exposure to these digital assets in a regulated, more familiar format. This led to the introduction of cryptocurrency ETFs.

Crypto ETFs aim to track the performance of one or more digital currencies, allowing investors to invest in cryptocurrencies without the challenges of direct ownership, such as storage and security concerns. The first Bitcoin ETFs, for instance, provided investors a simpler and regulated path to gain exposure to Bitcoin's price movements without owning the actual cryptocurrency. This innovation has significantly lowered the barriers to entry for investors interested in the cryptocurrency market but wary of its complexities and risks.

Conclusion

The historical context and evolution of ETFs and cryptocurrencies highlight a trajectory of financial innovation driven by market demand, technological advancements, and evolving investor needs. ETFs revolutionized the investment landscape with their simplicity and efficiency, while cryptocurrencies brought forth a new era of decentralized digital finance. The blend of these two, in the form of crypto ETFs, signifies a remarkable confluence of traditional and modern finance, opening new avenues for investment and portfolio diversification.

The Rise of Crypto ETFs

In the dynamic world of finance, the emergence of cryptocurrency Exchange-Traded Funds (ETFs) stands as a testament to the ever-evolving nature of investment strategies. This chapter explores the ascent of crypto ETFs, their impact on the market, and the reasons behind their growing popularity.

The Genesis of Crypto ETFs

The concept of crypto ETFs emerged from the desire to merge the burgeoning world of digital currencies with the regulated, more accessible framework of traditional investment vehicles. While cryptocurrencies offered a new frontier of digital assets, their complex nature, security concerns, and regulatory uncertainties posed challenges for mainstream investors. Crypto ETFs were developed as a solution, providing investors an opportunity to gain exposure to cryptocurrencies without the intricacies of buying, storing, and securing them directly.

Early Attempts and Regulatory Hurdles

The journey towards the establishment of crypto ETFs was not without challenges. The first proposals for Bitcoin ETFs were submitted to regulatory bodies like the U.S. Securities and Exchange Commission (SEC) as early as 2013. However, these early attempts faced significant setbacks, primarily due to concerns over market volatility, liquidity, custody, and potential market manipulation. Regulators were cautious, given the relatively untested and decentralized nature of cryptocurrencies.

Despite these initial rejections, the interest in crypto ETFs did not wane. The proponents of these products continued refining their approaches, addressing regulatory concerns, and advocating for the potential benefits of crypto ETFs in diversifying investment portfolios.

Breakthrough and Market Entry

The persistence paid off, and the first crypto ETFs began to emerge in various global markets. Countries like Canada and Brazil led the way, approving Bitcoin and Ethereum ETFs and setting a precedent for others to follow. These ETFs provided direct exposure to cryptocurrencies, with the underlying assets being physically held in secure custody.

In the United States, while the approval for a direct Bitcoin ETF remained elusive initially, investment firms found success with ETFs focused on blockchain technology companies. These ETFs invested in firms engaged in the research, development, support, or use of blockchain technology, indirectly exposing investors to the cryptocurrency sector.

The Impact and Appeal of Crypto ETFs

The introduction of crypto ETFs marked a significant milestone for both the cryptocurrency and ETF industries. For the traditional investor, crypto ETFs offered a familiar, regulated, and simpler way to invest in the volatile yet potentially lucrative world of digital currencies. These ETFs provided benefits like diversification, as cryptocurrencies often display low correlation with traditional asset classes like stocks and bonds.

For the cryptocurrency market, the approval and launch of crypto ETFs signified a step towards mainstream acceptance and recognition. It helped in demystifying digital currencies and attracted a broader investor base, including institutions that were previously hesitant to engage directly with cryptocurrencies.

Future Prospects

As the financial landscape continues to evolve, the rise of crypto ETFs reflects the market's adaptability and the growing demand for innovative investment products. The future of crypto ETFs seems promising, with ongoing efforts to launch more diverse products, including ETFs tracking multiple cryptocurrencies, and those offering different investment strategies like active management.

Conclusion

The ascent of crypto ETFs represents a pivotal development in bridging the gap between traditional finance and the novel world of digital currencies. By offering a regulated, accessible, and less complex way to invest in cryptocurrencies, these ETFs have not only expanded the investment horizon for many but also heralded a new era in the financial market, where innovation and adaptation continue to shape the future of investing.

The Role of Financial Advisors in Modern Wealth Management

In the ever-evolving landscape of modern wealth management, the role of financial advisors has become increasingly pivotal. This chapter explores how financial advisors are adapting to the complexities of today's financial markets, especially with the introduction of innovative products like cryptocurrency ETFs (Exchange-Traded Funds).

The primary role of financial advisors is to guide clients through the intricate world of investments, ensuring that their financial goals and risk tolerances are aligned with their investment strategies. In recent years, this role has expanded to encompass a more holistic approach to wealth management. Financial advisors now often find themselves navigating a broader array of investment options, complex regulatory environments, and rapidly evolving technological advancements.

The advent of digital assets, especially cryptocurrencies, has introduced a new asset class that demands both specialized knowledge and a keen understanding of its inherent volatility and regulatory uncertainties. Financial advisors are thus tasked with staying abreast of these developments to provide informed, strategic advice to clients who express interest in or could benefit from crypto investments, including crypto ETFs.

Moreover, financial advisors play a crucial role in educating clients about the potential risks and rewards associated with emerging investment vehicles. They must balance this with traditional wealth management strategies to ensure diversified portfolios that mitigate risks while aiming for optimal returns.

In the context of crypto ETFs, advisors must evaluate these products' fit within a client's portfolio, considering factors like investment horizon, risk appetite, and overall financial objectives. The ability to integrate new investment opportunities like crypto ETFs into traditional portfolio management is fast becoming a requisite skill for financial advisors in the modern financial era.

As the financial landscape continues to transform, financial advisors must continually adapt, educate themselves, and develop strategies that incorporate both traditional and contemporary investment avenues. This adaptability not only enhances their service offering but also positions them as valuable partners to clients navigating the complex world of investments.

The Evolving Landscape of Financial Advising

The domain of financial advising is witnessing a profound transformation, driven by technological advancements, changing market dynamics, and evolving client expectations. This chapter delves into these changes, illustrating how they are reshaping the role and strategies of financial advisors.

Technology: A Game Changer in Financial Advising

One of the most significant drivers of change in financial advising is technology. The advent of digital platforms, robo-advisors, and advanced analytical tools has revolutionized the way financial advice is delivered and consumed. Robo-advisors, employing algorithms to manage portfolios, offer low-cost, accessible investment advice, attracting tech-savvy, cost-conscious younger investors. Meanwhile, traditional advisors are increasingly leveraging technology to enhance their service offerings, using data analytics for more personalized advice and integrating digital communication tools to engage clients.

Shift in Investment Products and Strategies

The range of investment products has broadened substantially, with the emergence of complex financial instruments like derivatives, alternative investments, and most recently, cryptocurrencies and crypto ETFs. This diversification has compelled financial advisors to expand their expertise beyond traditional stocks and bonds. Advisors now need to understand a wider array of products to effectively meet their clients' diverse investment goals and risk appetites.

Regulatory Changes and Compliance

The regulatory landscape for financial advising is continuously evolving, with a growing emphasis on transparency and client protection. Regulations like the Department of Labor's Fiduciary Rule in the United States and the Markets in Financial Instruments Directive (MiFID) II in Europe have reshaped the advisor-client relationship, putting a premium on advisors' ability to demonstrate the value and suitability of their recommendations. Compliance has become a more significant aspect of the advisory role, requiring advisors to stay abreast of regulatory changes and ensure their practices adhere to the latest standards.

Changing Client Demographics and Expectations

The demographic profile of investors is changing. Millennials and Generation Z, who are beginning to constitute a larger portion of the investor base, have different financial goals and advising needs compared to Baby Boomers. They are more tech-savvy, socially conscious, and inclined towards ESG (Environmental, Social, and Governance) investing. These generational shifts necessitate a different advisory approach, one that is more aligned with these values and preferences.

The Growing Importance of Holistic Financial Planning

There is a noticeable shift from product-centric advising to a more holistic financial planning approach. Clients are increasingly seeking advice that integrates all aspects of their financial life, including retirement planning, tax strategies, estate planning, and even healthcare planning. This comprehensive approach requires advisors to possess a broader skill set and collaborate with other professionals like tax experts and estate lawyers.

Conclusion

The landscape of financial advising is evolving at an unprecedented pace. Financial advisors are adapting to these changes by embracing new technologies, expanding their knowledge base, complying with changing regulations, and responding to the diverse needs of a changing client demographic. This evolution is not just a challenge but an opportunity for advisors to enhance their value proposition, deepen client relationships, and play a pivotal role in their clients' financial well-being. As the industry continues to transform, the advisors who embrace change and continuously evolve are the ones who will thrive in this new era of financial advising.

The Importance of Understanding New Investment Tools

In an era marked by rapid financial innovation, the emergence of new investment tools has significantly altered the investment landscape. This chapter explores why understanding these tools is crucial for investors and financial advisors alike, highlighting the impact of such knowledge on investment strategies and client relationships.

Adapting to a Rapidly Changing Investment Environment

The financial market is constantly evolving, with new investment products and strategies being introduced regularly. From cryptocurrencies and blockchain technology to robo-advisors and algorithmic trading, the array of options available to investors is expanding at an unprecedented rate. Staying abreast of these developments is vital for investors and advisors to identify opportunities, manage risks, and maintain a competitive edge.

Enhanced Portfolio Diversification and Risk Management

One of the primary benefits of understanding new investment tools is the potential for improved portfolio diversification. Traditional portfolios typically focus on a mix of stocks, bonds, and cash. However, newer tools offer access to a wider range of asset classes, including digital assets, commodities, real estate, and more. By integrating these into investment strategies, investors can achieve a more robust diversification, potentially enhancing returns and reducing overall portfolio risk.

Meeting the Changing Needs and Expectations of Clients

The investor profile is changing, with a more diverse, informed, and tech-savvy clientele entering the market. These new investors often seek investments that align with their personal values, such as environmental, social, and governance (ESG) criteria, or are interested in the high-growth potential of innovative sectors like fintech or green technology. Advisors who understand and can navigate these new tools are better equipped to meet these evolving client preferences, leading to stronger and more enduring client relationships.

Navigating Regulatory Challenges and Compliance

As the investment landscape evolves, so does the regulatory environment. New investment tools often operate in grey areas of regulation or are subject to rapidly changing rules. Understanding these tools is not just about recognizing their potential but also about comprehending the associated regulatory requirements. This knowledge is critical for ensuring compliance and protecting clients from unforeseen legal or financial risks.

Leveraging Technology for Enhanced Investment Analysis

Advancements in technology have led to the development of sophisticated analytical tools, enabling deeper insights into market trends and asset performance. Proficiency in these technologies allows investors and advisors to conduct more comprehensive and accurate analyses, leading to better-informed investment decisions. It also enables the identification of emerging trends, providing an opportunity to capitalize on them early.

Staying Competitive in a Dynamic Market

In a market where new investment tools can quickly gain prominence, those who fail to keep pace risk being left behind. For financial advisors, in particular, their expertise and value proposition are often judged by their ability to navigate this complex and ever-changing environment. Embracing continuous learning and staying updated with new developments is essential for maintaining competitiveness and relevance in the industry.

Conclusion

Understanding new investment tools is crucial in today's dynamic financial landscape. It enables investors and advisors to enhance portfolio diversification, meet the evolving needs of clients, navigate regulatory complexities, leverage advanced technologies, and maintain competitiveness. As the financial world continues to evolve, this understanding will be key to seizing opportunities and achieving sustained success in the realm of investment.

Adapting to Client Interest in Cryptocurrencies

In recent years, the burgeoning interest in cryptocurrencies has become an unignorable trend in the world of finance. This chapter discusses how financial advisors and investors are adapting to this trend, emphasizing the significance of cryptocurrencies in modern investment portfolios and the strategies to navigate this new terrain.

Understanding the Surge in Cryptocurrency Popularity

The first step in adapting to client interest in cryptocurrencies is understanding the factors driving their popularity. Cryptocurrencies, spearheaded by Bitcoin, have garnered attention for their potential to offer high returns, decentralization, and innovation in financial transactions. The blockchain technology underlying these digital currencies promises security, transparency, and efficiency, appealing to a broad range of investors, from tech enthusiasts to those skeptical of traditional banking systems.

Educating Clients and Ourselves

Education is pivotal in adapting to the cryptocurrency trend. Many clients are drawn to cryptocurrencies due to media hype and the allure of rapid gains, often without a clear understanding of the risks and volatility involved. Financial advisors must educate themselves thoroughly on the intricacies of cryptocurrencies to provide informed advice. This education should encompass the technology behind digital currencies, the different types of cryptocurrencies available, their market dynamics, and potential regulatory changes.

Equally important is educating clients. Advisors should ensure that clients understand the high-risk nature of cryptocurrency investments, the potential for regulatory shifts, and the importance of considering these assets as part of a diversified portfolio rather than a standalone investment.

Integrating Cryptocurrencies into Investment Strategies

As interest in cryptocurrencies grows, advisors are increasingly tasked with determining how to incorporate these assets into traditional investment portfolios. This integration should be approached cautiously, considering the client's risk tolerance, investment horizon, and overall financial goals. For some clients, a small allocation to cryptocurrencies can add a layer of diversification to their portfolio. For others, particularly those with a lower risk tolerance or nearing retirement, the volatility of cryptocurrencies might not align with their investment objectives.

Navigating Regulatory and Security Challenges

The regulatory environment for cryptocurrencies is still in flux, which poses challenges for investors and advisors. Staying updated with regulatory changes and understanding the tax implications of cryptocurrency investments is crucial. Additionally, the security of digital assets is a significant concern. Advisors should guide clients on securing their investments, understanding the risks of digital wallets, and the importance of cybersecurity.

Leveraging Technology and New Investment Vehicles

To accommodate client interest in cryptocurrencies, advisors can leverage technology and new investment vehicles like cryptocurrency ETFs. These ETFs provide exposure to cryptocurrencies without the complexities of direct trading and storage, offering a more familiar and regulated investment pathway for traditional investors.

Conclusion

Adapting to client interest in cryptocurrencies requires a balanced approach, combining education, risk management, and an understanding of new investment vehicles. It's about guiding clients through the complexities of this new asset class, ensuring their investment decisions are well-informed and aligned with their overall financial goals.

Part I: Understanding Crypto ETFs

For financial professionals, grasping the basics of cryptocurrency ETFs (Exchange-Traded Funds) is essential in an era marked by rapid digital asset evolution. As clients increasingly express interest in the dynamic crypto market, advisors equipped with a comprehensive understanding of crypto ETFs are better positioned to offer informed guidance.

Understanding these instruments enables professionals to navigate their unique risks and opportunities effectively, ensuring well-rounded advice is provided. This knowledge is not just a tool for portfolio diversification but also a crucial aspect of staying relevant and competent in a financial landscape that increasingly intertwines with digital innovation and evolving investment paradigms.

What are Crypto ETFs?

Cryptocurrency Exchange-Traded Funds (ETFs) represent a novel and significant development in the financial markets, blending the innovation of digital currencies with the stability of traditional investment structures. This chapter demystifies Crypto ETFs, explaining their nature, functioning, and appeal to modern investors.

Defining Crypto ETFs

Crypto ETFs are investment funds traded on stock exchanges, much like traditional ETFs, but specifically designed to track the performance of one or more cryptocurrencies. They enable investors to invest in cryptocurrencies without the complexities of direct ownership, such as setting up digital wallets and navigating cryptocurrency exchanges. Instead, investors can buy and sell shares of the ETF through traditional brokerage accounts, just as they would with any other stock or ETF.

The Mechanism of Crypto ETFs

Crypto ETFs operate by either holding the underlying digital currencies directly (physical-backed) or using financial derivatives like futures contracts to mimic the performance of cryptocurrencies (synthetic). Physical-backed crypto ETFs purchase and hold the actual cryptocurrency, and the value of the ETF shares is directly tied to the price movements of the digital assets they hold. On the other hand, synthetic crypto ETFs use various financial instruments to emulate the price movements of cryptocurrencies, without holding the actual digital currencies.

Advantages of Investing in Crypto ETFs

1. **Accessibility and Simplicity**: Crypto ETFs offer a straightforward way for investors to gain exposure to the cryptocurrency market without dealing with the complexities and security concerns of buying and storing digital currencies.
2. **Diversification**: By investing in a basket of cryptocurrencies or companies involved in blockchain technology, crypto ETFs provide a diversified exposure to this sector, helping spread risk.
3. **Regulatory Compliance and Security**: Crypto ETFs are subject to regulatory oversight, providing a level of security and legitimacy that direct cryptocurrency investments may lack.
4. **Liquidity and Trading Flexibility**: Like other ETFs, crypto ETFs can be bought and sold during trading hours at market price, providing greater liquidity and flexibility compared to direct cryptocurrency investments.

Challenges and Risks

Despite their advantages, investing in crypto ETFs involves risks. The primary risk is market volatility, as cryptocurrencies are known for their sharp price fluctuations. Additionally, regulatory uncertainties continue to surround cryptocurrencies and, by extension, crypto ETFs. Investors must also consider the fund's expense ratios and management fees, which can impact returns.

Types of Crypto ETFs

Crypto ETFs can vary based on their investment focus. Some ETFs may track a single cryptocurrency, like Bitcoin or Ethereum, while others may track a basket of digital currencies. There are also ETFs that focus on blockchain technology companies, offering indirect exposure to the cryptocurrency market.

Conclusion

Crypto ETFs represent a significant step forward in the integration of digital currencies into mainstream financial markets. They offer a convenient, regulated, and flexible way for investors to tap into the potential of cryptocurrencies, albeit with inherent risks. As the cryptocurrency market continues to mature, it is likely that crypto ETFs will play an increasingly important role in the portfolios of forward-thinking investors, combining the innovation of digital assets with the familiarity and reliability of established financial structures.

How do Crypto ETFs Differ from Traditional ETFs?

While Crypto ETFs share some similarities with traditional ETFs, there are distinct differences that set them apart. Understanding these differences is crucial for investors and financial advisors to make informed decisions. This chapter explores how Crypto ETFs differ from their traditional counterparts in terms of underlying assets, market dynamics, regulatory environment, and investment strategies.

Underlying Assets: Digital vs. Physical

The most fundamental difference lies in the underlying assets. Traditional ETFs are typically based on a range of physical assets such as stocks, bonds, commodities, or a combination thereof. They may track well-established indices like the S&P 500 or specific sectors like technology, healthcare, or real estate.

Crypto ETFs, on the other hand, are based on digital assets – cryptocurrencies. These can be single-currency ETFs that track the performance of a particular cryptocurrency like Bitcoin or Ethereum, or they can be multi-currency ETFs that track a basket of cryptocurrencies. Some crypto ETFs also invest in companies involved in blockchain technology, offering indirect exposure to the crypto market.

Market Volatility and Risk Profile

Cryptocurrencies are known for their high volatility compared to traditional asset classes. This inherent volatility of the underlying assets makes crypto ETFs potentially more risky and unpredictable than traditional ETFs. The prices of cryptocurrencies can fluctuate wildly based on factors like technological changes, regulatory news, and market sentiment. This contrasts with the generally more stable and predictable markets for traditional assets like stocks and bonds.

Regulatory Environment

The regulatory framework for crypto ETFs is another area of difference. Traditional ETFs are well-entrenched within established regulatory environments, which have evolved over decades. In contrast, crypto ETFs operate in a newer, less defined regulatory space. The rules governing digital currencies are still in development in many jurisdictions, leading to a higher degree of uncertainty and regulatory risk for crypto ETFs.

Liquidity and Market Access

Liquidity can vary significantly between crypto and traditional ETFs. Traditional ETFs, especially those tracking major indices or sectors, typically enjoy high liquidity, making it easy for investors to buy and sell shares. However, the liquidity of crypto ETFs can be more variable, influenced by the liquidity of the underlying cryptocurrencies themselves and the market's perception of digital assets.

Investment Strategy and Portfolio Diversification

Investment strategies also differ. Traditional ETFs are often used for long-term investment strategies, like buy-and-hold, and are popular choices for diversifying portfolios due to the wide range of sectors and asset classes they cover. Crypto ETFs, while also used for diversification, often cater to a different investment strategy. They are frequently seen as a means to gain exposure to a high-growth, high-risk asset class. Investors may use them for shorter-term strategies or as a small proportion of a diversified portfolio to balance risk and return.

Conclusion

Understanding the differences between crypto ETFs and traditional ETFs is essential in the rapidly evolving world of investment. While they share the convenience and liquidity typical of ETF structures, the underlying assets, market dynamics, regulatory environment, and investment strategies present distinct characteristics and challenges. For investors, navigating these differences requires a balanced approach, considering both the innovative potential of crypto ETFs and the stability of traditional ETFs to achieve a well-rounded investment portfolio.

Types of Crypto ETFs Available

As the interest in cryptocurrencies continues to surge, the landscape of Crypto ETFs is expanding, offering investors a variety of ways to gain exposure to this novel asset class. This chapter outlines the different types of Crypto ETFs available, each catering to diverse investment strategies and risk appetites.

1. Single Cryptocurrency ETFs

Single cryptocurrency ETFs track the performance of one specific cryptocurrency, such as Bitcoin or Ethereum. These ETFs invest directly in the cryptocurrency they track, offering investors exposure to its price movements without the need for owning the digital currency directly. This type of ETF is ideal for investors who want to focus on the potential of a particular cryptocurrency but prefer the regulatory and operational framework of traditional securities.

2. Spot-Cryptocurrency ETFs (Spot bitcoin ETF)

At the time of writing this, the SEC has not yet given approval to any ETF that directly invests in cryptocurrency assets. Spot-bitcoin ETFs are specialized funds that directly track the current market price, or "spot" price, of Bitcoin. Unlike other investment vehicles that might use derivatives or futures contracts to emulate Bitcoin's value, spot-bitcoin ETFs hold actual Bitcoin. This approach offers investors real-time exposure to the fluctuations in Bitcoin's market price. These ETFs are ideal for those seeking to capitalize on the direct performance of Bitcoin while benefiting from the regulated and more accessible format of an ETF. This setup is particularly appealing to investors who prefer not to engage with the complexities and security concerns of handling Bitcoin directly.

3. Basket Cryptocurrency ETFs

Basket cryptocurrency ETFs hold a diversified portfolio of multiple cryptocurrencies. Instead of focusing on a single digital currency, these ETFs spread their investment across a range of cryptocurrencies, thereby diversifying the risk associated with any one digital asset. This type of ETF is suitable for investors looking to capitalize on the broader cryptocurrency market's growth potential rather than betting on a single currency.

3. Blockchain ETFs

Blockchain ETFs provide indirect exposure to the cryptocurrency market by investing in companies involved in the development and application of blockchain technology. This includes companies that use blockchain for financial transactions, supply chain management, or other purposes. Blockchain ETFs are an attractive option for investors who believe in the long-term potential of blockchain technology but want to avoid the direct volatility associated with cryptocurrencies.

4. Futures-Based Cryptocurrency ETFs

Futures-based cryptocurrency ETFs do not invest directly in cryptocurrencies; instead, they invest in futures contracts of digital currencies. These ETFs aim to track the performance of cryptocurrencies through futures markets, offering a different risk and return profile compared to ETFs that hold cryptocurrencies directly. They are a choice for investors comfortable with the complexities of futures trading and looking for a regulated way to speculate on cryptocurrency prices.

5. Actively Managed Cryptocurrency ETFs

Unlike most traditional ETFs that are passively managed, actively managed cryptocurrency ETFs involve portfolio managers actively making decisions about which digital assets to hold and when to buy or sell them. These ETFs aim to outperform a benchmark index by leveraging the expertise of the management team. They are suitable for investors who prefer having professionals manage their cryptocurrency investments and are willing to pay potentially higher fees for active management.

6. Leveraged and Inverse Cryptocurrency ETFs

Leveraged and inverse cryptocurrency ETFs are designed for short-term trading strategies. Leveraged ETFs seek to deliver multiples of the daily performance of the cryptocurrency they track, while inverse ETFs aim to deliver the opposite of the daily performance. These ETFs use financial derivatives and debt to achieve their goals and are generally considered high-risk investment vehicles.

7. Brief List of Currently Available Crypto ETFs

The following brief list is a snapshot of the options available for incorporating digital assets into the investment portfolios.

- **ProShares Bitcoin Strategy ETF**
- **ProShares Short Bitcoin Strategy ETF**
- **ProShares Ether Strategy ETF**
- **Bitwise Bitcoin and Ether Equal Weight Strategy**
- **Bitwise Bitcoin Strategy Optimum Roll ETF**
- **Valkyrie Bitcoin and Ether Strategy ETF**
- **ARK 21 Shares Active Bitcoin Futures Strategy ETF**
- **ARK 21 Shares Active Ethereum Futures Strategy ETF**

Conclusion

The variety of Crypto ETFs available reflects the growing sophistication of the cryptocurrency investment landscape. From single-currency ETFs to futures-based and actively managed funds, each type of Crypto ETF offers different levels of exposure, risk, and potential returns. For investors and financial advisors, understanding these options is key to navigating the complex world of digital asset investments and making informed decisions that align with investment goals and risk tolerance. As the market for cryptocurrencies evolves, so too will the range and nature of Crypto ETFs, providing even more avenues for portfolio diversification and exposure to this cutting-edge asset class.

Regulatory Landscape for Crypto ETFs

Current Regulations Surrounding Crypto ETFs

The regulatory landscape for cryptocurrency Exchange-Traded Funds (ETFs) is an evolving and critical aspect of their development and adoption. This chapter explores the current regulatory environment for crypto ETFs, highlighting key regulatory frameworks and their implications for investors and financial advisors.

Understanding the Regulatory Framework

The regulation of crypto ETFs varies significantly across different jurisdictions, reflecting the diverse approaches governments and financial regulators take towards cryptocurrencies and digital assets. Generally, regulatory bodies are concerned with investor protection, market integrity, and preventing financial crimes like money laundering and fraud.

In the United States, the Securities and Exchange Commission (SEC) plays a pivotal role in regulating ETFs, including those based on cryptocurrencies. The SEC's primary concerns revolve around market manipulation, liquidity, valuation, and custody of the underlying digital assets. Despite these concerns, the U.S. saw its first Bitcoin futures-based ETFs approved in 2021, marking a significant regulatory milestone.

Other countries have taken different approaches. For example, Canada and several European countries have been more receptive, approving several crypto ETFs that directly hold cryptocurrencies. These ETFs are subject to strict regulatory guidelines, ensuring proper risk disclosure, asset custody, and compliance with existing financial regulations.

Key Regulatory Considerations

1. **Market Manipulation and Volatility**: Regulators are concerned about the potential for market manipulation in the relatively nascent and less regulated cryptocurrency markets. This concern is heightened by the significant price volatility observed in these markets.

2. **Custody and Security of Assets**: Ensuring the secure custody of digital assets is a critical regulatory focus. Crypto ETFs must demonstrate robust mechanisms to safeguard these assets against theft, hacking, and other cybersecurity risks.

3. **Transparency and Disclosure**: Regulators require thorough disclosure of risks associated with crypto ETFs to investors. This includes clarity on pricing, valuation methods, and the specifics of the underlying assets.

4. **Compliance with Anti-Money Laundering (AML) and Know Your Customer (KYC) Norms**: Given the pseudonymous nature of cryptocurrencies, crypto ETFs are scrutinized for compliance with AML and KYC regulations.

The Impact of Regulations on Investors and Advisors

For investors and financial advisors, understanding these regulatory nuances is crucial. It affects the availability, risk profile, and suitability of crypto ETFs as investment options. Advisors must keep abreast of regulatory changes to provide compliant and up-to-date advice to clients interested in cryptocurrency investments.

Future Regulatory Trends

The regulatory environment for crypto ETFs is expected to continue evolving as the market matures and as regulators gain a deeper understanding of cryptocurrencies. This evolution could lead to more standardized regulatory frameworks, potentially opening the door for a wider range of crypto ETF offerings, including those holding cryptocurrencies directly.

Conclusion

The current regulatory landscape for crypto ETFs is complex and varied, reflecting the ongoing efforts of regulators to balance innovation with investor protection. For those engaged in the financial markets, staying informed about these regulations is essential. As the market for digital assets grows and matures, so too will the regulatory frameworks that govern them, shaping the future of crypto ETF investments. Understanding these regulatory dynamics is critical for investors and advisors looking to navigate this emerging asset class responsibly and effectively.

How Regulations Impact Investment Strategies

Regulatory frameworks play a pivotal role in shaping investment strategies, particularly in emerging markets like cryptocurrencies and crypto ETFs. This chapter delves into the ways in which regulations influence investment decision-making, risk management, and the overall approach to portfolio construction.

1. Setting the Boundaries for Investment Choices

Regulations fundamentally determine what is permissible in the investment world. For cryptocurrencies and crypto ETFs, regulatory stances vary significantly across different countries, influencing both the availability and the characteristics of these investment options. In jurisdictions where crypto ETFs are heavily regulated or not permitted, investors may have to seek alternative routes, like investing in individual cryptocurrencies or blockchain technology stocks, or using international trading platforms. Conversely, in countries with clear and supportive regulations, a broader range of crypto investment products, including various types of crypto ETFs, becomes available.

2. Influencing Risk Assessment

Regulations are often designed to protect investors from excessive risk. They can mandate disclosures, set standards for asset custody and security, and enforce measures against market manipulation. For investors and financial advisors, understanding these regulatory protections helps in assessing the risk profile of crypto investments. It can influence decisions such as the proportion of crypto assets in a portfolio and the selection between different types of crypto ETFs (e.g., physically-backed vs. futures-based).

3. Compliance and Due Diligence

Investment strategies must also consider compliance with regulatory requirements, including anti-money laundering (AML) and know-your-customer (KYC) laws. These regulations necessitate thorough due diligence on the part of both investors and advisors, impacting the time and resources allocated to investment analysis and decision-making processes. The need for compliance shapes investment strategies, potentially favoring products and markets with clearer and more stable regulatory environments.

4. Impact on Liquidity and Market Dynamics

Regulatory frameworks can significantly impact market liquidity. Stringent regulations might limit market participation, thereby affecting the liquidity of certain crypto assets or ETFs. On the other hand, clear and supportive regulations can enhance market liquidity by attracting a broader base of investors. Investment strategies need to account for these liquidity considerations, as they affect the ability to enter and exit positions and manage portfolio volatility.

5. Taxation and Its Implications

Taxation regulations regarding crypto assets vary globally and can significantly affect investment returns. Different tax treatments for capital gains from crypto investments, rules regarding tax events (like crypto-to-crypto trades), and differing tax rates for different types of crypto assets can all influence investment strategies. Investors and advisors need to structure their crypto investments in a tax-efficient manner, aligning their strategies with the prevailing tax laws.

6. Anticipating Regulatory Changes

Finally, the rapidly evolving nature of cryptocurrency regulations requires a proactive approach to investment strategy. Investors and advisors need to anticipate potential regulatory changes and their implications. This might involve staying flexible in investment choices, being prepared to adjust portfolio allocations quickly, or employing hedging strategies to mitigate regulatory risks.

Conclusion

Regulations play a crucial and multifaceted role in shaping investment strategies in the crypto space. From determining permissible investment avenues to influencing risk assessment, compliance, market dynamics, and taxation, regulatory considerations are integral to responsible and effective investment decision-making. For investors and financial advisors, navigating these regulatory landscapes is key to developing robust, compliant, and successful investment strategies in the dynamic world of cryptocurrencies and crypto ETFs.

Future Regulatory Trends

As the cryptocurrency and crypto ETF markets continue to evolve, so too does the regulatory landscape surrounding them. This chapter explores potential future regulatory trends in this space, shedding light on how these anticipated changes could shape the market and influence investment strategies.

1. Increased Global Regulatory Coordination

One of the key trends likely to emerge is increased global regulatory coordination. As cryptocurrencies operate on a global scale, disjointed regulatory approaches can lead to inefficiencies and market manipulation risks. In response, international regulatory bodies, such as the Financial Action Task Force (FATF) and the International Monetary Fund (IMF), may play a more significant role in establishing global standards for cryptocurrency regulation. This coordination could lead to more uniform regulatory practices, which would provide clarity to investors and reduce compliance burdens for global financial institutions.

2. Enhanced Consumer Protection Measures

Protecting investors will continue to be a primary focus of regulators. Future trends may include stricter consumer protection measures, such as enhanced disclosure requirements for crypto ETFs, standardized risk assessment criteria for cryptocurrency investments, and tighter controls over crypto advertising. These measures aim to ensure that investors are well-informed about the risks associated with crypto investments and are protected from deceptive practices.

3. Clarification and Standardization of Taxation Rules

Another area of focus is likely to be the clarification and standardization of taxation rules for cryptocurrencies and related investment products. As governments seek to incorporate crypto assets into their tax frameworks, investors can expect more explicit guidelines on how these assets are taxed, including rules for capital gains, income generation, and inheritance. This would reduce uncertainty and complexity for investors and financial advisors in managing tax liabilities.

4. Strengthening Anti-Money Laundering (AML) and Know Your Customer (KYC) Regulations

Given the pseudonymous nature of cryptocurrencies, strengthening AML and KYC regulations will be a key area of development. Regulators may introduce more rigorous checks and balances for crypto exchanges and wallet providers. This could include enhanced monitoring of transactions, stricter identity verification processes, and increased reporting requirements. These measures aim to prevent the use of cryptocurrencies for illicit activities while ensuring the integrity of financial markets.

5. Institutionalization and Custody Solutions

As institutional interest in cryptocurrencies grows, regulators are likely to establish clearer guidelines for institutional participation. This may include specific regulations around custody solutions, ensuring that institutional holdings of digital assets meet high security and compliance standards. Such regulations would not only provide a safer environment for institutional investors but also increase overall market stability.

6. Recognition and Regulation of Decentralized Finance (DeFi)

Decentralized Finance (DeFi) is a rapidly growing sector within the crypto market, and its regulation is still in nascent stages. Future regulatory trends may involve the formal recognition and regulation of DeFi platforms and products. This would involve navigating the decentralized and non-custodial nature of these platforms, balancing innovation with investor protection.

Conclusion

Anticipating future regulatory trends is crucial for investors and financial advisors involved in the cryptocurrency and crypto ETF markets. These trends point towards a future where the regulatory environment is more harmonized, transparent, and conducive to protecting investors while supporting market growth. Staying informed and adaptable in the face of these regulatory changes will be key to navigating the complexities of this evolving landscape and capitalizing on the opportunities it presents.

Risks and Rewards of Crypto ETFs

Investing in cryptocurrency ETFs presents a blend of risks and rewards, reflecting the volatile nature of digital assets. On the rewards side, crypto ETFs offer investors an innovative avenue for portfolio diversification and exposure to the high growth potential of cryptocurrencies without the complexities of direct trading and storage. However, these rewards come with significant risks. The primary risk is market volatility, with crypto markets known for rapid and unpredictable price swings. Additionally, regulatory uncertainties and evolving technological landscapes add layers of complexity. Investors must balance these risks against the potential rewards, aligning their investment strategies with their risk tolerance and financial goals.

Volatility and Risk Management in Cryptocurrency Investments

The world of cryptocurrency is renowned for its high volatility, which, while offering potential for substantial returns, also presents significant risks. This chapter examines the nature of this volatility and outlines strategies for effective risk management in cryptocurrency investments, including crypto ETFs.

Understanding the Volatility in Cryptocurrencies

Cryptocurrency markets are characterized by rapid and significant price fluctuations. This volatility can be attributed to several factors:

1. **Market Maturity**: Compared to traditional financial markets, the cryptocurrency market is relatively young and still evolving, which contributes to price instability.
2. **Market Sentiment**: Cryptocurrencies are highly susceptible to market sentiment, often influenced by media coverage, public statements by influential individuals, or regulatory news.
3. **Liquidity**: Many cryptocurrencies have lower market liquidity compared to traditional assets, leading to more significant price changes in response to large trades.
4. **Technological Developments**: Advances or setbacks in blockchain technology, security breaches, and changes in network protocols can swiftly impact cryptocurrency prices.

Risk Management Strategies

1. **Diversification**: One of the key strategies to manage risk in any investment portfolio is diversification. In the context of cryptocurrencies, this could mean diversifying across different cryptocurrencies, as well as holding a mix of traditional and digital assets. Crypto ETFs, especially those that track a basket of cryptocurrencies or blockchain-related companies, can be an effective tool for achieving this diversification.
2. **Position Sizing**: Given the high risk associated with cryptocurrencies, it is prudent to limit the size of cryptocurrency investments within the overall portfolio. A conservative approach might involve allocating a smaller percentage of the total investment capital to these assets.
3. **Regular Review and Rebalancing**: Due to the rapid changes in the cryptocurrency market, regular review and rebalancing of the portfolio are

essential. This helps in maintaining the desired asset allocation and risk level, adjusting for changes in market value.

4. **Understanding and Acceptance of Risk**: Investors should have a clear understanding of the risks involved in cryptocurrency investments, including the possibility of losing their entire investment. This level of risk acceptance should be aligned with the individual's investment goals, time horizon, and overall risk tolerance.

5. **Use of Stop-Loss Orders**: To mitigate the risk of large losses, investors can use stop-loss orders, which automatically sell an asset when its price falls to a certain level. This tool can be particularly useful in managing the downside risk of volatile markets.

6. **Staying Informed**: Keeping abreast of market trends, technological developments, and regulatory changes can aid investors in making more informed decisions and anticipating market movements.

7. **Seeking Professional Advice**: For those unfamiliar with the complexities of the cryptocurrency market, seeking advice from financial professionals who understand these assets can be beneficial.

Conclusion

While the volatility of cryptocurrencies can present attractive opportunities for high returns, it also necessitates robust risk management strategies. By understanding the factors driving this volatility and employing sound investment practices, such as diversification, careful position sizing, regular portfolio review, and informed decision-making, investors can navigate these turbulent markets more effectively. As the cryptocurrency market continues to evolve, so too must the strategies employed to manage the risks associated with these dynamic and innovative assets.

Potential Returns and Growth Opportunities in Cryptocurrency Investments

Cryptocurrency investments, characterized by their high volatility, also offer the potential for substantial returns and growth opportunities. This chapter delves into the factors contributing to these prospects and how investors can navigate this space to capitalize on these opportunities.

Understanding the High Return Potential

Cryptocurrency markets have garnered attention for their rapid price appreciation over a relatively short period. Early adopters of cryptocurrencies like Bitcoin have witnessed exponential returns, with the value of some digital currencies soaring to unprecedented highs. Several factors contribute to this high return potential:

1. **Innovation and Technology Adoption**: As blockchain technology continues to evolve and gain acceptance, cryptocurrencies that leverage this technology are poised for growth. The potential for widespread adoption in various sectors, from finance to supply chain management, creates opportunities for significant appreciation in value.

2. **Market Sentiment and Investor Interest**: The growing interest and investment in cryptocurrencies by both retail and institutional investors can drive up prices. Media attention and public endorsements by high-profile individuals and companies often fuel investor enthusiasm, leading to rapid price increases.

3. **Limited Supply and Increasing Demand**: Many cryptocurrencies have a capped supply, most notably Bitcoin with its 21 million coin limit. This limited supply, combined with increasing demand, can lead to higher prices.

4. **Diversification into New Asset Classes**: For investors looking to diversify their portfolios beyond traditional assets like stocks, bonds, and commodities, cryptocurrencies offer an alternative investment class with a low correlation to other markets.

Growth Opportunities Beyond Direct Investment

1. **Crypto ETFs and Index Funds**: For those wary of the complexities of direct cryptocurrency trading, crypto ETFs and index funds provide a more accessible route. These investment vehicles offer exposure to a range of cryptocurrencies, reducing the reliance on the performance of a single digital currency.

2. **Blockchain Technology Investments**: Investing in companies that are developing or adopting blockchain technology offers indirect exposure to the growth of the cryptocurrency market. These companies range from startups in the fintech sector to established tech giants exploring blockchain applications.

3. **Emerging Cryptocurrency Sectors**: Sectors within the cryptocurrency market, such as Decentralized Finance (DeFi) and Non-Fungible Tokens (NFTs), present new growth avenues. These emerging sectors have their own set of risks but also offer innovative investment opportunities in the evolving digital asset landscape.

Balancing Risk and Reward

While the potential for high returns is a compelling aspect of cryptocurrency investments, it comes with considerable risk. The market is prone to sudden and substantial price swings, and regulatory uncertainties add to the risk profile. Investors must balance the lure of high returns with a thorough understanding of these risks. This involves not only researching and understanding the market but also employing prudent investment strategies, such as diversification and risk management techniques discussed in earlier chapters.

Conclusion

The potential returns and growth opportunities in the cryptocurrency market are significant, driven by technological innovation, market dynamics, and the evolving landscape of digital assets. However, navigating this market requires a careful balance of risk and reward. Investors must approach these opportunities with a well-informed and strategic mindset, recognizing the high-risk nature of these assets while exploring the diverse avenues for growth and returns they offer.

Diversification Benefits of Cryptocurrency Investments

Diversification is a cornerstone of sound investment strategy, aimed at reducing risk by spreading investments across various asset classes. In recent years, cryptocurrencies and related financial products like crypto ETFs have emerged as a new asset class, offering unique diversification benefits. This extended chapter examines these benefits, considering the distinct characteristics of cryptocurrencies and how they can complement traditional investment portfolios.

Understanding Portfolio Diversification

Portfolio diversification involves investing in a range of assets to reduce the risk associated with any single investment. A well-diversified portfolio typically includes a mix of stocks, bonds, commodities, and, increasingly, alternative investments like real estate, private equity, and now, digital assets like cryptocurrencies. The key to effective diversification is choosing assets with low correlation to each other, meaning their prices do not move in tandem.

Cryptocurrencies as a Distinct Asset Class

Cryptocurrencies have emerged as a distinct asset class, primarily due to their underlying technology, market dynamics, and growth potential. Unlike traditional assets, their market movements are not strongly correlated with conventional financial markets. This lack of correlation is partly because cryptocurrency markets are influenced by factors unique to digital assets, such as technological developments, adoption rates, regulatory changes, and market sentiment specific to cryptocurrencies.

Benefits of Including Cryptocurrencies in Investment Portfolios

1. **Enhanced Diversification**: The low correlation of cryptocurrencies with traditional assets like stocks and bonds can help in reducing overall portfolio volatility. By adding cryptocurrencies or crypto ETFs to a portfolio, investors can potentially smooth out returns during periods when traditional markets are underperforming.

2. **High Growth Potential**: Cryptocurrencies have shown the potential for high returns, albeit with higher risk. For investors willing to tolerate this risk, a small allocation to cryptocurrencies can significantly enhance the growth potential of their portfolio.

3. **Inflation Hedge**: Some investors view Bitcoin and other cryptocurrencies as a hedge against inflation and currency devaluation. The decentralized nature and limited supply of many cryptocurrencies make them attractive in environments where traditional currency values are falling.

4. **Access to Emerging Technologies and Markets**: Investing in cryptocurrencies or blockchain-focused ETFs provides exposure to innovative blockchain technology and its potential applications across various industries.

Risk Considerations and Balanced Approach

While the diversification benefits are compelling, it's important to approach cryptocurrency investments with caution:

1. **Market Volatility**: Cryptocurrencies are known for their high volatility, with prices capable of significant swings in short periods. This volatility can add risk to a portfolio, even if the overall correlation with other assets is low.
2. **Regulatory Risks**: The regulatory environment for cryptocurrencies is still evolving, which can add uncertainty and risk to these investments.
3. **Operational Risks**: Issues related to the storage and security of digital assets, as well as the operational integrity of cryptocurrency exchanges, need to be considered.
4. **Knowledge and Understanding**: Investors need to have a good understanding of the cryptocurrency market, the technology behind it, and the specific assets they are investing in.

Strategies for Incorporating Cryptocurrencies for Diversification

1. **Allocating a Small Portfolio Percentage**: Given the high risk, a conservative approach is to allocate a relatively small percentage of the overall portfolio to cryptocurrencies.
2. **Using Crypto ETFs**: For those who prefer not to invest in cryptocurrencies directly, crypto ETFs offer a more regulated and straightforward way to gain exposure to this asset class.
3. **Regular Monitoring and Rebalancing**: Given the dynamic nature of the cryptocurrency market, regular monitoring and rebalancing are essential to maintain desired risk levels.
4. **Diversification within Cryptocurrency Investments**: Within the cryptocurrency allocation, diversifying across different cryptocurrencies or blockchain technologies can further spread risk.

Conclusion

Cryptocurrencies present a unique opportunity for portfolio diversification, offering potential benefits like low correlation with traditional asset classes, high growth potential, and inflation hedge properties. However, the inherent risks associated with this volatile and evolving market necessitate a cautious and well-informed approach. By carefully considering the allocation size, leveraging vehicles like crypto ETFs, and staying informed about market developments, investors can harness the diversification benefits of cryptocurrencies while managing the associated risks. As the digital asset space continues to mature, its role in portfolio diversification strategies is likely to become increasingly significant, offering a new dimension to traditional investment paradigms.

Part II: Integrating Crypto ETFs into Client Portfolios

Client Profiling and Suitability

Determining client suitability for cryptocurrency ETFs is a critical responsibility for financial advisors. Given the unique characteristics of crypto ETFs, including high volatility and evolving regulatory frameworks, they may not be suitable for all investors. Advisors must carefully evaluate each client's risk tolerance, investment horizon, and financial goals. Clients with a higher risk appetite and a long-term investment perspective may find crypto ETFs a suitable addition to diversify their portfolio. Conversely, conservative investors or those with short-term financial objectives might be advised to limit or avoid exposure to these high-risk assets. Tailoring advice to individual client profiles is key in responsibly incorporating crypto ETFs into investment strategies.

Assessing Client Risk Tolerance in the Context of Cryptocurrency Investments

In the realm of financial advising, accurately gauging a client's risk tolerance is critical, especially when considering the inclusion of volatile assets like cryptocurrencies in their portfolio. This chapter discusses the importance of assessing risk tolerance and strategies to effectively evaluate and incorporate it into investment decisions, particularly in the context of cryptocurrency investments.

Understanding Risk Tolerance

Risk tolerance is the degree of variability in investment returns that an investor is willing to withstand. It's influenced by several factors, including the investor's financial goals, investment horizon, financial stability, and emotional comfort with risk. In the context of cryptocurrencies, which are known for their high volatility, assessing risk tolerance becomes even more crucial.

Factors Influencing Risk Tolerance in Cryptocurrency Investing

1. **Investment Time Horizon**: Clients with a longer investment horizon may be more suited to withstand the volatility of cryptocurrency investments, as they have more time to recover from potential downturns.
2. **Financial Goals**: Understanding a client's financial goals is essential. Clients investing for long-term goals like retirement may have different risk tolerances compared to those seeking short-term gains.
3. **Financial Situation and Stability**: A client's overall financial health, including income stability, debt levels, and emergency savings, can significantly impact their ability to tolerate risk.
4. **Experience with Investments**: Clients who are experienced investors and familiar with market fluctuations may be more comfortable with the risks associated with cryptocurrencies.
5. **Emotional Response to Volatility**: Some clients may be more emotionally equipped to handle the stress of market fluctuations typical of cryptocurrency markets.

Methods to Assess Risk Tolerance

1. **Questionnaires and Surveys**: Utilizing detailed questionnaires or surveys can help gauge a client's risk tolerance. These tools can cover aspects like investment experience, reaction to hypothetical market scenarios, and understanding of the risks involved in cryptocurrency investments.
2. **Behavioral Analysis**: Observing past investment behaviors and decisions can provide insights into a client's risk tolerance. Advisors should consider how clients have reacted to previous market downturns and their investment decision-making patterns.
3. **Ongoing Conversations**: Regular discussions about market conditions, investment performance, and financial goals can help advisors continually assess and understand their client's risk tolerance.

4. **Educational Approaches**: Educating clients about the nature of cryptocurrency markets, the potential for high volatility, and long-term perspectives can aid in making informed decisions aligned with their risk tolerance.

Incorporating Risk Tolerance into Investment Strategies

Once risk tolerance is assessed, it's crucial to integrate this understanding into investment strategies:

1. **Customized Portfolio Allocation**: For clients interested in cryptocurrency investments, advisors should tailor the portfolio allocation based on their risk tolerance, ensuring that exposure to cryptocurrencies aligns with their ability to absorb risk.
2. **Diversification**: Encourage diversification within the cryptocurrency portion of their portfolio, spreading investments across various types of crypto assets and related investments, like crypto ETFs.
3. **Regular Reviews and Adjustments**: Continuously monitor and adjust cryptocurrency investments as market conditions change and as clients' risk tolerance evolves over time.

Conclusion

Assessing client risk tolerance is a fundamental aspect of financial advising, especially with the inclusion of high-risk assets like cryptocurrencies. An accurate understanding of a client's risk profile, combined with ongoing education and communication, allows for the development of a tailored investment strategy that aligns with their financial goals and comfort with risk. As the cryptocurrency market continues to evolve, so too must the approaches to evaluating and integrating risk tolerance in investment planning.

Matching Client Profiles with Appropriate Crypto ETFs

In the dynamic world of cryptocurrency investments, selecting the right crypto ETFs for clients involves a nuanced understanding of both the client's profile and the diverse range of ETF options available. This chapter explores how financial advisors can effectively match their clients with the most suitable crypto ETFs, aligning with their financial goals, risk tolerance, and investment preferences.

Understanding Client Profiles

Client profiles are unique composites of various factors, including:

1. **Investment Goals**: Whether a client is seeking long-term growth, income, or capital preservation can significantly influence the choice of crypto ETFs.

2. **Risk Tolerance**: This encompasses how much market volatility a client is willing and able to endure, which is particularly pertinent in the high-risk environment of cryptocurrencies.

3. **Investment Horizon**: Clients with a longer investment horizon may be better positioned to handle the volatility associated with crypto investments compared to those looking for short-term gains.

4. **Financial Knowledge and Experience**: Clients who are more knowledgeable and experienced with investment concepts, especially with cryptocurrencies, might be more comfortable with complex and volatile crypto ETFs.

5. **Liquidity Needs**: Clients with higher liquidity needs may require more cautious investment in crypto ETFs, considering the potential volatility of these assets.

Types of Crypto ETFs and Client Suitability

1. **Single Cryptocurrency ETFs**: Suitable for clients who wish to focus on the potential of a specific cryptocurrency, like Bitcoin or Ethereum. These are for clients who may have a stronger conviction about the prospects of a particular digital currency.

2. **Basket Cryptocurrency ETFs**: Ideal for clients looking to diversify their cryptocurrency exposure. These ETFs mitigate the risk of investing in a single cryptocurrency by spreading investments across a range of digital currencies.

3. **Blockchain Technology ETFs**: Appropriate for clients interested in the broader applications of blockchain technology, beyond just cryptocurrencies. These ETFs invest in companies developing or utilizing blockchain technology and are suited for clients seeking exposure to this sector's growth potential.

4. **Actively Managed Crypto ETFs**: Best for clients who prefer professional management in the rapidly changing cryptocurrency market. These ETFs may involve higher fees but can offer the advantage of expert portfolio management.

Assessing and Recommending Suitable Crypto ETFs

1. **Educating Clients**: Advisors should educate clients about the different types of crypto ETFs, including their risk profiles, underlying assets, and investment strategies.

2. **Analyzing Financial Profiles**: Advisors need to conduct a thorough analysis of each client's financial profile, considering their goals, risk tolerance, investment horizon, and knowledge level.

3. **Customizing Recommendations**: Based on the analysis, advisors can tailor their recommendations, suggesting specific crypto ETFs that align with the client's profile.

4. **Reviewing and Adjusting Over Time**: Client profiles and market conditions can change over time. Regular reviews of the client's portfolio and adjusting ETF holdings as necessary are crucial.

Conclusion

Matching client profiles with appropriate crypto ETFs requires a deep understanding of both the client's specific financial needs and goals and the diverse range of crypto ETFs available. By carefully assessing each client's profile and educating them about the nuances of different ETF options, advisors can help clients navigate the complex world of cryptocurrency investing. This tailored approach ensures that clients invest in crypto ETFs that align with their individual risk tolerances, investment horizons, and overall financial strategies.

Educating Clients About Crypto ETFs

In the rapidly evolving world of financial investments, cryptocurrencies and their associated products, like crypto ETFs, have become a topic of significant interest. For many clients, however, the complexities of these products can be daunting. This chapter discusses strategies for financial advisors to effectively educate their clients about crypto ETFs, ensuring they are well-informed and comfortable with these novel investment vehicles.

Understanding the Need for Education

The cryptocurrency market, characterized by its volatility and the technical nature of its products, presents a steep learning curve. Crypto ETFs, while simplifying investment in digital currencies, still carry inherent risks and complexities that clients need to understand. Effective education can help demystify these products, aiding clients in making informed investment decisions.

Key Areas of Focus in Client Education

1. **Basics of Cryptocurrency and Blockchain**: Start with the fundamentals of cryptocurrencies and blockchain technology. Explain what cryptocurrencies are, how they work, the idea of decentralization, and the role of blockchain technology.

2. **What Are Crypto ETFs**: Clearly define what crypto ETFs are and how they differ from direct cryptocurrency investments. Explain the types of crypto ETFs available, such as those investing directly in cryptocurrencies, those based on futures contracts, and those focusing on blockchain technology companies.

3. **Risks and Volatility**: Emphasize the volatile nature of the cryptocurrency market and how it impacts crypto ETFs. Discuss the risks involved, including market volatility, regulatory changes, and technological risks.

4. **Potential Benefits and Drawbacks**: Outline both the potential benefits, such as portfolio diversification and access to a new asset class, and the drawbacks, like higher expense ratios and the uncertainty of new financial products.

5. **Regulatory Environment**: Provide an overview of the current regulatory landscape for crypto ETFs, highlighting how it might differ from traditional ETFs and the implications for investors.

6. **Tax Implications**: Discuss the tax considerations of investing in crypto ETFs, noting any differences from traditional investment products.

Strategies for Effective Education

1. **Use Simple and Relatable Language**: Avoid jargon and technical terms. Use analogies and simple language to explain complex concepts.

2. **Tailor the Education to the Client**: Adjust the depth and breadth of information based on the client's existing knowledge, interest, and investment experience.

3. **Provide Educational Resources**: Offer clients access to educational materials like articles, videos, and infographics that they can review in their own time.

4. **Regular Updates and Discussions**: Keep clients informed about the latest developments in the crypto market and regulatory changes. Encourage ongoing discussions to address any questions or concerns they may have.

5. **Interactive Learning Experiences**: Use tools like webinars, workshops, or interactive financial planning software to engage clients actively in the learning process.

Conclusion

Educating clients about crypto ETFs is a crucial aspect of financial advising in the modern investment landscape. By providing clear, comprehensive, and tailored education, advisors can empower their clients to make informed decisions about these novel investment products. This education process not only builds client trust and confidence but also ensures that clients are better equipped to understand the risks and potential rewards associated with investing in crypto ETFs.

Portfolio Construction with Crypto ETFs

Incorporating cryptocurrency ETFs into portfolio construction requires strategic planning to balance risk and opportunity. Given their volatile nature, crypto ETFs should typically represent a modest proportion of the overall portfolio, complementing more traditional asset classes to enhance diversification. Financial advisors need to carefully assess each client's risk tolerance, investment goals, and time horizon when determining the appropriate allocation to crypto ETFs. A well-structured portfolio with crypto ETFs can offer exposure to the potential high returns of digital currencies while mitigating risk through broader asset diversification, thus aligning with the client's long-term investment strategy and risk appetite.

Strategic Asset Allocation in the Context of Crypto ETFs

Strategic asset allocation is a fundamental approach in investment management, focusing on setting target allocations for various asset classes based on an investor's goals, risk tolerance, and investment horizon. This chapter explores the incorporation of cryptocurrency Exchange-Traded Funds (ETFs) into the strategic asset allocation process, considering the unique attributes of these innovative investment vehicles.

Understanding Strategic Asset Allocation

Strategic asset allocation involves creating an asset mix that aims to balance risk and return in line with an investor's long-term objectives. This typically involves a diversified portfolio comprising different asset classes such as stocks, bonds, real estate, and increasingly, alternative investments like cryptocurrencies.

The Role of Crypto ETFs in Asset Allocation

1. **Diversification Benefit**: Crypto ETFs represent a relatively new asset class with low correlation to traditional asset classes, offering diversification benefits that can potentially reduce overall portfolio volatility.

2. **Growth Potential**: Given their historical performance, cryptocurrencies can offer substantial growth potential. Crypto ETFs allow investors to tap into this growth while mitigating some of the risks associated with direct cryptocurrency investments.

3. **Risk Considerations**: Crypto assets are known for their high volatility, which must be factored into the asset allocation process. The allocation to crypto ETFs should be in line with the investor's risk tolerance and capacity.

4. **Long-term Perspective**: Considering the nascent and highly speculative nature of cryptocurrencies, any allocation to crypto ETFs should be made with a long-term perspective, acknowledging the potential for significant fluctuations in the short term.

Incorporating Crypto ETFs into Strategic Asset Allocation

1. **Assessing Investor Profile**: Determine the investor's financial goals, risk tolerance, and investment horizon. This assessment will guide how much of the portfolio should be allocated to crypto ETFs.

2. **Allocation Size**: For most investors, especially those with a low to moderate risk tolerance, crypto ETFs should represent a relatively small portion of the overall portfolio to manage risk effectively.

3. **Selection of Crypto ETFs**: Choose the appropriate type of crypto ETF based on the investor's profile and investment goals. This could range from ETFs focusing on a single cryptocurrency to those offering a diversified exposure to multiple digital currencies or blockchain technology stocks.

4. **Regular Review and Rebalancing**: Due to the high volatility of crypto markets, regular portfolio reviews and rebalancing are crucial to maintain the desired asset allocation over time.

5. **Tax Considerations**: Be aware of the tax implications of investing in crypto ETFs, as they might differ from those of traditional investments.

Conclusion

Incorporating crypto ETFs into strategic asset allocation requires a nuanced approach that balances the potential high returns of this emerging asset class with its inherent risks. A well-thought-out allocation to crypto ETFs can enhance portfolio diversification and growth potential, but it must be carefully calibrated to align with the individual investor's overall investment strategy and risk profile. As the cryptocurrency market continues to evolve, so too will its role in strategic asset allocation, offering both challenges and opportunities to investors seeking to optimize their portfolios for long-term success.

Tactical Asset Allocation with Crypto ETFs

Tactical asset allocation is an active management strategy that adjusts the investment mix in a portfolio to capitalize on market inefficiencies or economic conditions. This chapter discusses the integration of cryptocurrency Exchange-Traded Funds (ETFs) into a tactical asset allocation strategy, focusing on how these innovative assets can be leveraged for short-term opportunities while aligning with long-term investment objectives.

Understanding Tactical Asset Allocation

Tactical asset allocation involves short-term adjustments to an investment portfolio's asset mix, deviating from the original strategic asset allocation to take advantage of market opportunities or to hedge against imminent risks. This approach requires a more hands-on investment style and a deep understanding of market trends and economic indicators.

The Role of Crypto ETFs in Tactical Asset Allocation

1. **Market Responsiveness**: Crypto ETFs provide an efficient vehicle for quickly responding to market changes in the cryptocurrency sector. Their ease of trading on traditional exchanges allows for rapid portfolio adjustments.
2. **Leveraging Volatility**: The inherent volatility of cryptocurrencies can be a double-edged sword. While it introduces higher risk, it also presents opportunities for tactical gains. Skilled investors can use crypto ETFs to capitalize on these price fluctuations.
3. **Hedging Against Inflation or Currency Devaluation**: Some investors view cryptocurrencies, particularly Bitcoin, as a hedge against inflation or fiat currency devaluation. Tactical allocation to crypto ETFs can be used as a short-term hedge in certain economic conditions.

4. **Exposure to Emerging Trends**: The crypto market is continually evolving, with new trends emerging regularly (e.g., DeFi, NFTs). Tactical asset allocation allows investors to gain exposure to these trends through targeted crypto ETFs.

Strategies for Incorporating Crypto ETFs into Tactical Asset Allocation

1. **Market Analysis and Timing**: Successful tactical asset allocation with crypto ETFs requires a keen analysis of market trends and timing. Investors need to stay informed about developments in both the cryptocurrency and broader financial markets.

2. **Diversification within Crypto Assets**: Within the cryptocurrency allocation, tactical diversification can be achieved by investing in different types of crypto ETFs, balancing between single-currency ETFs, diversified crypto ETFs, and blockchain technology ETFs.

3. **Risk Management**: Given the high-risk nature of cryptocurrencies, tactical allocation should involve strict risk management protocols, including setting stop-loss orders and position sizing rules.

4. **Flexibility and Adaptability**: Being flexible and ready to adapt to changing market conditions is crucial. This means regularly reviewing the portfolio and being prepared to make swift adjustments.

5. **Alignment with Long-Term Objectives**: While tactical asset allocation focuses on short-term adjustments, it is essential to ensure that these changes remain aligned with the investor's long-term financial goals and risk tolerance.

Conclusion

Integrating crypto ETFs into a tactical asset allocation strategy offers investors an avenue to potentially enhance returns and manage risks through active portfolio management. This approach, while more hands-on and requiring a greater understanding of market dynamics, can allow investors to capitalize on the unique opportunities presented by the cryptocurrency market. However, it is important to approach this strategy with a disciplined risk management approach and a clear view of how short-term tactical decisions fit within the broader, long-term investment strategy.

Portfolio Rebalancing Strategies with Crypto ETFs

Portfolio rebalancing is an essential strategy for maintaining the desired asset allocation over time, especially in the context of volatile assets like cryptocurrency ETFs. This chapter outlines effective rebalancing strategies, ensuring that portfolios including crypto ETFs remain aligned with investors' risk tolerance and investment objectives.

Understanding the Importance of Rebalancing

Rebalancing involves adjusting the weights of different assets in a portfolio back to their target allocations. This process is crucial because over time, as some investments outperform others, the portfolio can become overexposed to certain assets, leading to a risk profile that may not align with the investor's initial strategy. Given the high volatility of cryptocurrencies, portfolios including crypto ETFs can quickly become misaligned, making rebalancing a critical practice.

Rebalancing Strategies in Portfolios with Crypto ETFs

1. **Time-Based Rebalancing**: This approach involves rebalancing at regular intervals, such as quarterly, semi-annually, or annually. Time-based rebalancing is straightforward and can help in systematically reducing the risk of overexposure to crypto ETFs due to their potential rapid growth.
2. **Threshold-Based Rebalancing**: Here, rebalancing occurs when an asset's allocation deviates by a certain percentage from its target allocation. Given the volatility of crypto ETFs, setting a tighter threshold for these assets can be prudent.
3. **Combination Approach**: Some investors may opt for a combination of time and threshold-based strategies, rebalancing at regular intervals but also when allocations deviate beyond set thresholds.

Considerations for Rebalancing with Crypto ETFs

1. **Tax Implications**: Rebalancing can trigger tax consequences, especially for taxable accounts. Selling assets that have appreciated in value may result in capital gains taxes. Careful planning and consideration of tax-efficient rebalancing strategies are important.

2. **Transaction Costs**: Consider the transaction costs associated with rebalancing, including any fees for buying or selling assets. Efficient rebalancing minimizes these costs.

3. **Market Conditions and Volatility**: The high volatility of crypto ETFs requires a nuanced approach to rebalancing. Rapid and significant price changes in these ETFs may necessitate more frequent monitoring and potentially more frequent rebalancing.

4. **Alignment with Investment Goals and Risk Profile**: Ensure that the rebalancing strategy keeps the portfolio aligned with the investor's long-term goals and risk tolerance. Rebalancing should not be a reactionary measure to short-term market movements but a strategic decision to maintain the desired asset allocation.

Tools and Techniques for Efficient Rebalancing

1. **Automated Rebalancing Tools**: Many investment platforms offer automated rebalancing tools that can help investors stick to their rebalancing strategy without manual intervention.

2. **Cash Flows for Rebalancing**: Using dividends, interest income, or new contributions to rebalance the portfolio can be a tax-efficient strategy. This involves using this cash to purchase underweighted assets, rather than selling overweighted assets, which could incur taxes.

3. **Rebalancing through Crypto ETF Selection**: Choose the appropriate type of crypto ETF (e.g., diversified vs. single cryptocurrency) based on the current market conditions and the portfolio's need for rebalancing.

Conclusion

Rebalancing is a vital process in portfolio management, especially when dealing with volatile assets like crypto ETFs. Regular and strategic rebalancing helps ensure that the portfolio remains aligned with the investor's goals, risk tolerance, and investment strategy. By carefully considering factors such as tax implications, transaction costs, and market conditions, investors can implement effective rebalancing strategies that maintain the health and balance of their investment portfolios.

Performance Monitoring and Reporting

Effective performance monitoring and reporting are crucial for managing cryptocurrency ETF investments. Due to the inherent volatility of crypto markets, advisors should conduct frequent and thorough performance reviews of crypto ETF holdings. This involves assessing not only the returns but also understanding how these investments affect the overall risk profile of the portfolio. Regular reporting to clients is essential to maintain transparency and trust, providing clear information on performance metrics, market changes, and potential impacts on investment goals. Accurate and timely reporting aids clients in making informed decisions and assists advisors in adjusting strategies to align with evolving market conditions.

Tracking the Performance of Crypto ETFs

As cryptocurrency Exchange-Traded Funds (ETFs) gain popularity, understanding how to effectively track their performance becomes crucial for investors and financial advisors. This chapter outlines strategies for monitoring the performance of crypto ETFs, providing insights into their role in investment portfolios and the broader market context.

Understanding Crypto ETF Performance Metrics

Tracking the performance of crypto ETFs involves more than just looking at price changes. It includes a variety of metrics such as:

1. **Total Return**: This measures the ETF's performance over time, accounting for both capital gains and any distributions, such as dividends or interest.

2. **Comparison to Benchmark Indices**: Comparing the ETF's performance to relevant cryptocurrency indices or a basket of cryptocurrencies can provide context to its relative performance.

3. **Expense Ratios and Fees**: Understanding the costs associated with the ETF, including management fees and operational expenses, is essential as they can significantly impact net returns.

4. **Trading Volume and Liquidity**: Monitoring trading volumes helps assess the liquidity of the ETF, which can impact the ease of entering and exiting positions.

5. **Tracking Error**: This metric shows how closely the ETF follows its benchmark index, which is especially important for index-tracking crypto ETFs.

Tools and Resources for Performance Tracking

1. **Financial News and Analysis Platforms**: Utilize financial news websites and analysis platforms that provide real-time data and expert analysis on crypto ETFs.

2. **Investment Portfolio Management Software**: Many software tools offer features to track and analyze the performance of individual investments, including crypto ETFs, within a broader portfolio.

3. **Crypto Market-Specific Resources**: Given the unique nature of cryptocurrencies, specialized crypto market tracking tools can provide in-depth analysis relevant to crypto ETFs.

4. **Regular Reports from ETF Providers**: ETF issuers typically provide regular reports on performance, holdings, and other relevant metrics, which can be a valuable resource for investors.

Incorporating Performance Tracking into Investment Decisions

1. **Aligning with Investment Goals**: Regular tracking allows investors to ensure that the performance of crypto ETFs aligns with their investment objectives, whether it's growth, income, or diversification.

2. **Risk Management**: By keeping an eye on performance trends and volatility, investors can make informed decisions to manage risk, such as rebalancing the portfolio or adjusting exposure to crypto ETFs.

3. **Market Trend Analysis**: Performance tracking can offer insights into broader market trends, helping investors understand the market cycles and sentiment in the cryptocurrency space.

Challenges in Tracking Crypto ETFs

1. **Market Volatility**: The high volatility of cryptocurrencies can lead to rapid and significant fluctuations in ETF performance, requiring more frequent monitoring.

2. **Emerging Market Dynamics**: As the crypto market is relatively new and evolving, historical data may be limited, making it challenging to predict future performance based on past trends.

3. **Regulatory Changes**: The crypto market is susceptible to regulatory changes, which can have sudden and significant impacts on performance.

Conclusion

Effectively tracking the performance of crypto ETFs is essential for informed investment management. By utilizing a range of tools and resources and understanding key performance metrics, investors can gain valuable insights into how these ETFs are performing and how they fit within their overall investment strategy. Regular performance tracking, combined with a deep understanding of the unique characteristics of the crypto market, enables investors to make strategic decisions, manage risks, and capitalize on the opportunities presented by this emerging asset class.

Effective Reporting to Clients on Crypto ETF Investments

Transparent and comprehensive reporting is a cornerstone of client trust and satisfaction in financial advisory. With the increasing inclusion of cryptocurrency ETFs (Exchange-Traded Funds) in investment portfolios, advisors must adapt their reporting practices to effectively communicate the performance and implications of these novel assets. This chapter focuses on strategies for reporting on crypto ETF investments to clients.

Understanding the Unique Reporting Needs for Crypto ETFs

Crypto ETFs, given their relative novelty and volatility, require a tailored approach in reporting. Clients may not be as familiar with these assets as they are with traditional investments. Therefore, reports need to be educational, clear, and thorough, providing clients with a comprehensive understanding of their crypto ETF holdings and their impact on overall portfolio performance.

Key Elements of Reporting on Crypto ETFs

1. **Performance Metrics**: Include detailed performance data for crypto ETFs, such as total return, price fluctuations, and comparison against relevant benchmarks or sectors.

2. **Market Context**: Given the volatile nature of cryptocurrencies, it's important to provide context for the performance. This may include market trends, regulatory updates, and technological advancements in the blockchain space.

3. **Risk Assessment**: Clearly communicate the risks associated with crypto ETF investments, including market volatility, regulatory changes, and potential technological issues.

4. **Expense Ratios and Fees**: Detail all costs associated with the crypto ETFs, as fees can significantly impact net returns.

5. **Allocation and Diversification Impact**: Explain how crypto ETFs fit into the client's overall portfolio strategy, particularly in terms of asset allocation and diversification.

6. **Tax Implications**: Report on any tax implications related to trading or holding crypto ETFs, as the tax treatment may differ from more traditional assets.

Best Practices for Reporting to Clients

1. **Clarity and Simplicity**: Use clear and straightforward language to explain complex concepts. Visual aids like charts and graphs can be particularly effective in illustrating performance trends and portfolio allocations.

2. **Customization**: Tailor reports to the individual needs and understanding levels of each client. Some may require more detailed explanations, particularly if they are less familiar with cryptocurrency as an asset class.

3. **Frequency and Timing**: Determine the appropriate frequency of reports based on the volatility of crypto ETFs and the client's preferences. Some clients may appreciate more frequent updates due to the fast-moving nature of the crypto market.

4. **Interactive Reporting Tools**: Consider using digital platforms that allow clients to interact with their reports, such as through dynamic charts or personalized dashboards.

5. **Educational Component**: Include an educational section in reports to help clients understand the broader cryptocurrency market and its potential impact on their investments.

6. **Consistency with Overall Reporting**: Ensure that reporting on crypto ETFs is integrated seamlessly with the overall portfolio reporting, maintaining a consistent format and style.

Conclusion

Effective reporting on crypto ETF investments is crucial in helping clients understand and feel comfortable with these assets in their portfolios. By focusing on clarity, context, and comprehensive information, financial advisors can enhance client understanding and confidence in their investment strategies. As the cryptocurrency market continues to evolve, so too should the strategies for reporting on these assets, ensuring that clients are always well-informed and aligned with their investment objectives.

Adjusting Investment Strategies Based on Crypto ETF Performance

Investing in cryptocurrency Exchange-Traded Funds (ETFs) introduces a dynamic element into a portfolio, requiring ongoing assessment and potential adjustments to investment strategies. This chapter explores how investors and financial advisors can adapt their strategies based on the performance of crypto ETFs, ensuring that these investments continue to align with overall financial goals and risk tolerance.

Understanding the Impact of Crypto ETF Performance

Crypto ETFs, reflecting the inherent volatility of the cryptocurrency market, can exhibit significant fluctuations in performance. This volatility can affect the overall risk profile of an investment portfolio, making it essential to continuously evaluate and adjust strategies as needed.

Key Considerations for Strategy Adjustments

1. **Performance Analysis**: Regularly analyze the performance of crypto ETFs in the context of the entire portfolio. This includes assessing not just returns, but also how these assets influence the portfolio's volatility and risk exposure.
2. **Market Trends and Developments**: Stay informed about the latest trends and developments in the cryptocurrency market, including regulatory changes, technological advancements, and market sentiment shifts. These factors can significantly impact the performance of crypto ETFs.
3. **Rebalancing**: Given the high volatility of crypto ETFs, more frequent rebalancing may be necessary to maintain the desired asset allocation. This process involves selling portions of overperforming assets and buying underperforming ones to realign with the target allocation.
4. **Risk Management**: Continuously assess the risk that crypto ETFs bring to the portfolio, especially during periods of high volatility. If necessary, adjust the allocation to ensure that the level of risk remains within the client's comfort zone.

5. **Diversification Strategies**: If a particular crypto ETF shows sustained underperformance or increased risk, consider diversifying within the cryptocurrency asset class. This can include investing in different types of crypto ETFs or combining direct cryptocurrency investments with ETFs.

6. **Tax Considerations**: Be mindful of the tax implications when adjusting investment strategies. Realizing gains or losses can have tax consequences that should be factored into decision-making.

Strategies for Adjusting Based on Performance

1. **Incremental Adjustments**: Make small, incremental changes to the investment in crypto ETFs rather than large, reactive shifts. This approach can prevent overreaction to short-term market movements.

2. **Performance Thresholds**: Set performance thresholds that trigger a review of the investment strategy. For instance, if a crypto ETF's value changes by a certain percentage, it could prompt a reevaluation of its role in the portfolio.

3. **Long-Term Perspective**: Maintain a long-term perspective when adjusting strategies. Cryptocurrency markets can be prone to short-term hype or panic, so it's important to focus on long-term objectives and fundamentals.

4. **Utilizing Stop-Loss Orders**: Implement stop-loss orders to limit potential losses on crypto ETFs. This risk management tool automatically sells the ETF if its price falls below a specified level.

Conclusion

Adjusting investment strategies based on the performance of crypto ETFs is a critical aspect of managing a modern investment portfolio. By regularly analyzing performance, staying informed about market developments, and maintaining a disciplined approach to rebalancing and risk management, investors can ensure that their exposure to crypto ETFs remains in line with their investment objectives and risk tolerance.

Part III: Advanced Strategies and Considerations

Tax Implications of Investing in Crypto ETFs

Investing in cryptocurrency ETFs carries unique tax implications that investors must consider. Similar to traditional ETFs, crypto ETFs are subject to capital gains taxes when sold at a profit. The tax rate depends on whether gains are classified as short-term or long-term, based on the holding period. Additionally, any dividends or interest earned from these ETFs are typically taxable. Since crypto ETFs are a relatively new investment vehicle, the tax regulations surrounding them can be complex and subject to change. Investors should consult with tax professionals to understand these implications fully and ensure compliance with current tax laws.

Understanding Tax Treatment of Crypto ETF Investments

Navigating the tax implications of cryptocurrency ETFs (Exchange-Traded Funds) is a crucial aspect of investment strategy. This chapter provides an overview of the tax considerations for crypto ETFs, helping investors and financial advisors make informed decisions that optimize tax efficiency.

Basic Tax Principles for Crypto ETFs

Like any investment, crypto ETFs are subject to taxation, but the novel nature of cryptocurrencies introduces specific tax considerations. The tax treatment of crypto ETFs can vary depending on the jurisdiction, the structure of the ETF, and the investor's tax status.

Capital Gains Tax

1. **Realized Gains and Losses**: When an investor sells shares of a crypto ETF, any profit made is typically subject to capital gains tax. The rate can vary based on the length of time the shares were held (short-term vs. long-term capital gains).

2. **Tax Reporting**: Investors are responsible for reporting gains and losses on their tax returns. Detailed record-keeping of transactions, including purchase and sale prices and dates, is crucial for accurate reporting.

Dividends and Distributions

1. **Tax on Distributions**: Some crypto ETFs may distribute dividends to shareholders, which are usually subject to income tax. The tax rate can depend on whether the dividends are qualified or non-qualified.

2. **Reinvested Dividends**: Dividends that are automatically reinvested to purchase more shares of the ETF are still taxable in the year they are received.

ETF Structure and Tax Efficiency

1. **Physical vs. Synthetic ETFs**: The tax treatment can differ based on the ETF's structure. Physical crypto ETFs (holding actual cryptocurrencies) and synthetic crypto ETFs (using derivatives) may have different tax implications.

2. **ETF Domicile**: The country in which the ETF is domiciled can impact its tax treatment. Investors should be aware of any tax treaties or international tax laws that may apply.

Tax Considerations for International Investors

Non-resident investors in crypto ETFs may be subject to different tax rules. This can include withholding taxes on dividends and differing treatment of capital gains. Understanding the tax laws of both the investor's home country and the country where the ETF is based is essential.

Tax Planning Strategies

1. **Holding Period**: Consider the holding period for crypto ETFs to potentially qualify for lower long-term capital gains rates.
2. **Tax-Loss Harvesting**: This involves selling underperforming assets to realize losses, which can offset realized capital gains and reduce tax liability.
3. **Account Type**: Investing in crypto ETFs through tax-advantaged accounts (like IRAs or 401(k)s in the U.S.) can offer tax benefits, as gains and dividends may grow tax-deferred or tax-free.

Staying Informed on Regulatory Changes

The regulatory landscape for cryptocurrencies and related investment products is evolving. Keeping abreast of changes in tax laws and regulations is crucial for effective tax planning and compliance.

Conclusion

Understanding the tax treatment of crypto ETF investments is essential for effective portfolio management and tax planning. By considering the tax implications of buying, holding, and selling these assets, and employing strategic tax planning, investors can optimize the after-tax returns of their crypto ETF investments. As the cryptocurrency market continues to mature, staying informed and seeking professional tax advice will be key to navigating the complexities of this emerging asset class.

Tax-Efficient Investing Strategies for Crypto ETFs

Investing in cryptocurrency ETFs (Exchange-Traded Funds) not only involves understanding the market dynamics but also necessitates a strategic approach to tax efficiency. Effective tax management can significantly impact the net returns of crypto ETF investments. This chapter discusses various strategies to maximize tax efficiency for investors engaging with crypto ETFs.

1. Understanding the Tax Implications of Crypto ETFs

Before delving into strategies, it's crucial to comprehend the tax implications specific to crypto ETFs. Depending on the jurisdiction, gains from crypto ETFs might be subject to capital gains tax, and the treatment of dividends or distributions from these ETFs could vary. Knowing these details will help in planning a tax-efficient investment strategy.

2. Utilizing Tax-Advantaged Accounts

Investing in crypto ETFs through tax-advantaged accounts can be a smart strategy. For instance, in the United States, using accounts like Individual Retirement Accounts (IRAs) or 401(k)s can offer deferred or tax-free growth. Contributions to these accounts may reduce taxable income, and the investments can grow tax-free until withdrawal.

3. Holding Period Considerations

Long-term capital gains tax rates are generally lower than short-term rates in many jurisdictions. By holding crypto ETFs for a period that qualifies them as long-term investments (usually over a year), investors can benefit from these lower rates.

4. Tax-Loss Harvesting

This involves selling underperforming investments to realize losses, which can then offset gains in other areas of the portfolio. If crypto ETFs have declined in value, selling them can help offset the taxes on gains from other investments, thereby reducing the overall tax liability.

5. Asset Location Strategy

This strategy involves placing investments in the most tax-efficient accounts available. For example, holding crypto ETFs in taxable accounts might be more beneficial if they qualify for lower long-term capital gains rates, while keeping high-dividend or interest-bearing investments in tax-advantaged accounts.

6. Rebalancing with Tax Efficiency in Mind

Rebalancing is essential for maintaining the desired asset allocation in a portfolio. Doing this in a tax-efficient manner involves considering the tax implications of selling certain assets. Where possible, rebalancing through new contributions or using dividends and interest can be more tax-efficient than selling assets.

7. Keeping Abreast of Tax Law Changes

Tax laws, especially concerning emerging asset classes like cryptocurrencies, can evolve. Staying informed about these changes is crucial to maintaining a tax-efficient strategy. This might involve regular consultations with a tax professional who is knowledgeable about the latest developments in cryptocurrency taxation.

8. Consideration of State and Local Taxes

In addition to federal taxes, state and local taxes can also impact investment returns. Understanding these additional tax liabilities is important for a comprehensive approach to tax-efficient investing.

Conclusion

Adopting tax-efficient investing strategies for crypto ETFs is critical for optimizing returns. This involves a multi-faceted approach that includes understanding the specific tax implications of crypto ETFs, utilizing tax-advantaged accounts, considering holding periods, implementing tax-loss harvesting, strategically locating assets, and rebalancing with a focus on tax implications. Additionally, staying informed about changing tax laws and considering local tax implications are essential aspects of a comprehensive tax-efficient investment strategy. By incorporating these elements, investors can significantly enhance the overall efficiency and performance of their crypto ETF investments.

Global Perspectives on Crypto ETFs: Embracing Digital Assets Across Borders

The adoption and integration of cryptocurrency ETFs (Exchange-Traded Funds) in investment portfolios are not uniform across the globe. This chapter explores how different countries are embracing crypto ETFs, highlighting the varying regulatory landscapes, investor sentiments, and market developments in the burgeoning world of digital asset investing.

1. United States: Cautious Approach with Regulatory Hurdles

In the United States, the journey towards embracing crypto ETFs has been cautious and regulatory-driven. The Securities and Exchange Commission (SEC) has been meticulous in its approach, primarily concerned with market manipulation, liquidity, and investor protection. While several proposals for Bitcoin and other crypto ETFs have been submitted, the SEC has been slow to approve them, citing concerns over market volatility and regulatory compliance. However, the U.S. has seen the introduction of Bitcoin futures ETFs, which marks a significant step forward in the acceptance of crypto-related investment products.

2. Canada: A Pioneer in Crypto ETF Approvals

Canada has been a pioneer in approving crypto ETFs, showcasing a more progressive stance. The Ontario Securities Commission approved the first Bitcoin ETF in North America, followed by approvals for Ethereum ETFs and others. These ETFs offer direct exposure to cryptocurrencies and are seen as a major breakthrough in providing investors with more regulated and accessible means to invest in digital currencies.

3. Europe: Varied Approaches with Growing Interest

European countries have shown varied approaches to crypto ETFs, with some nations being more receptive than others. In countries like Germany and Switzerland, investors have access to a range of crypto investment products, including ETFs and ETPs (Exchange-Traded Products). These products are listed on established stock exchanges and have attracted significant interest from both retail and institutional investors.

4. Asia-Pacific: Diverse Regulatory Environments

The Asia-Pacific region presents a diverse picture. Countries like Australia are exploring the possibility of crypto ETFs, with regulatory bodies cautiously assessing the risks and benefits. Meanwhile, in countries like Japan and South Korea, regulatory challenges and concerns over investor protection have slowed the adoption of crypto ETFs. However, there is growing interest and demand among investors, indicating potential developments in the future.

5. Latin America and Other Emerging Markets

In Latin America and other emerging markets, the interest in crypto ETFs is growing, driven by high adoption rates of cryptocurrencies among the population. Brazil, for instance, has seen the launch of its own Bitcoin ETF, indicating a growing acceptance of digital assets in investment portfolios.

6. Regulatory Harmonization and Future Trends

One of the key trends in the global embrace of crypto ETFs is the potential for regulatory harmonization. As international regulatory bodies communicate and collaborate, there may be more consistent and clear regulations for crypto ETFs. This could lead to increased availability and uniformity of these products across different markets.

Conclusion

The global perspective on crypto ETFs reflects the diversity and complexity of embracing digital assets in regulated investment products. While countries like Canada and some in Europe have taken the lead, others like the United States and those in the Asia-Pacific region are moving more cautiously. The future of crypto ETFs will likely be shaped by a combination of regulatory evolution, investor demand, and market innovations, reflecting the dynamic and global nature of cryptocurrency investing. As countries continue to adapt and refine their approaches, crypto ETFs are poised to become an increasingly integral part of the global investment landscape.

Exploring Opportunities in Global Crypto ETF Markets

The global landscape for cryptocurrency Exchange-Traded Funds (ETFs) presents a diverse array of opportunities for investors. This chapter delves into the evolving opportunities in the global crypto ETF markets, examining the different approaches of various countries and regions, and how these create unique investment prospects.

1. The Pioneering North American Market

North America, particularly the United States and Canada, has been at the forefront of developing the crypto ETF market. While the U.S. has been cautious, primarily offering Bitcoin futures-based ETFs, Canada has emerged as a leader by approving several crypto ETFs that hold actual cryptocurrencies. This pioneering approach offers investors opportunities for direct exposure to cryptocurrencies, with the added benefits of regulated, traditional investment structures.

2. Europe's Diverse Crypto ETF Landscape

Europe presents a diverse market for crypto ETFs, with countries like Germany and Switzerland leading in offering a range of crypto investment products. These include ETFs and Exchange-Traded Products (ETPs) that provide exposure to various cryptocurrencies. The European market's openness to digital asset ETFs offers investors opportunities for diversification and access to innovative financial products.

3. The Growth in the Asia-Pacific Region

The Asia-Pacific region, although varied in its approach to crypto ETFs, is showing signs of growth. Countries like Australia are exploring crypto ETFs, and there is burgeoning interest in Japan and South Korea, despite regulatory hesitancy. The region's high rate of cryptocurrency adoption among the population could drive the future growth of crypto ETF markets here, presenting new opportunities for investors.

4. Emerging Markets and Latin America's Foray into Crypto ETFs

Emerging markets, particularly in Latin America, have shown a high interest in cryptocurrencies. Brazil, for example, has launched its own Bitcoin ETF, indicating a growing acceptance of digital assets in investment portfolios. These markets offer unique opportunities as they could leverage crypto ETFs to attract global investors and provide local investors with regulated investment options in cryptocurrencies.

5. Regulatory Developments and Innovations

Globally, regulatory developments in the crypto space are critical to shaping investment opportunities. Countries that establish clear and favorable regulations for crypto ETFs could attract significant investment. Additionally, innovations in ETF structures and the introduction of new products catering to specific cryptocurrencies or blockchain technologies could open up novel investment avenues.

6. Institutional Involvement and Market Maturity

As the global crypto ETF market matures, increased institutional involvement is likely. This could bring more stability and credibility to these investment products, making them more attractive to a broader range of investors. The entry of institutional players could also lead to more varied and sophisticated crypto ETF offerings.

Conclusion

The opportunities in the global crypto ETF markets are as diverse as they are dynamic. From the pioneering efforts in North America and Europe to the growing interest in Asia-Pacific and emerging markets, the global landscape offers a range of investment opportunities. As regulatory frameworks evolve and markets mature, crypto ETFs are set to become an increasingly integral part of the global investment ecosystem, offering new ways for investors to engage with digital assets.

Future Trends and Innovations

The financial market is on the cusp of a transformative era, driven by rapid technological advancements and evolving investor preferences. Future trends point towards the increased integration of artificial intelligence and machine learning for personalized investment strategies and market analysis. Blockchain technology is expected to gain further traction, revolutionizing transaction methods and enhancing security. The rise of decentralized finance (DeFi) will continue to challenge traditional financial models, offering innovative lending and trading platforms. Moreover, sustainable and socially responsible investing (SRI) will become more prominent, as investors increasingly seek to align their portfolios with environmental and social values. These trends signify a shift towards a more technologically integrated, ethical, and user-centric financial landscape.

Emerging Trends in Cryptocurrency and ETF Markets

The cryptocurrency and Exchange-Traded Fund (ETF) markets are at the forefront of financial innovation, continuously evolving with new trends and developments. This chapter explores the emerging trends in these markets, offering insights into how they are shaping the future of investing.

1. Decentralized Finance (DeFi) Integration

One of the most significant trends in the cryptocurrency market is the rise of Decentralized Finance (DeFi). DeFi platforms offer financial services, including lending, borrowing, and trading, without traditional intermediaries, using blockchain technology. This innovation is beginning to influence the ETF market, with the potential for DeFi-focused ETFs offering investors exposure to this cutting-edge sector.

2. Increased Institutional Adoption

Cryptocurrencies, once the domain of individual enthusiasts, are seeing increased interest from institutional investors. Large financial institutions and corporations are either investing directly in cryptocurrencies or in related investment products like ETFs. This institutional adoption is likely to drive the development of more diversified and sophisticated crypto ETFs, catering to the needs of these large-scale investors.

3. Expansion of Blockchain ETFs

Blockchain technology underpins cryptocurrencies but has applications far beyond digital currencies. ETFs focusing on blockchain technology invest in companies developing or utilizing this technology. As blockchain finds more applications in sectors like supply chain management, healthcare, and finance, the scope and variety of blockchain ETFs are expected to expand.

4. Regulatory Evolution and Clarity

The cryptocurrency market's regulatory environment is rapidly evolving, with significant implications for crypto ETFs. As governments and financial authorities around the world develop clearer and more consistent regulations, this could lead to increased investor confidence and the launch of new crypto ETF products in markets that were previously hesitant.

5. Growth in Niche Cryptocurrency ETFs

As the market matures, there is a trend towards the development of niche cryptocurrency ETFs. These ETFs focus on specific segments of the cryptocurrency market, such as particular types of digital currencies (like privacy coins or utility tokens) or specific blockchain applications. This specialization allows investors to tailor their exposure according to their interests and beliefs about future market developments.

6. Integration of ESG Principles

Environmental, Social, and Governance (ESG) investing principles are becoming increasingly important in the ETF market. In the crypto space, this trend is manifesting in concerns about the environmental impact of cryptocurrency mining and the social implications of blockchain technology. Future crypto ETFs may focus more on sustainability and ESG compliance, attracting a new segment of socially conscious investors.

7. Technological Advancements in Trading and Security

Advancements in technology are continuously shaping the cryptocurrency and ETF markets. Innovations in trading platforms, enhanced security measures for digital asset custody, and the integration of artificial intelligence for market analysis are some of the trends that could influence the trading and management of crypto ETFs.

Conclusion

The intersection of cryptocurrency and ETF markets is a hotbed of innovation and growth, driven by trends like DeFi integration, institutional adoption, expansion of blockchain ETFs, regulatory evolution, niche market development, ESG integration, and technological advancements. For investors and financial advisors, staying abreast of these trends is crucial for navigating this dynamic landscape and capitalizing on the emerging opportunities in the world of digital assets and investment products.

Anticipating Potential Future Products and Services in the Crypto ETF Space

The rapidly evolving domain of cryptocurrency and ETFs holds immense potential for future innovations in products and services. As technology advances and market acceptance grows, we can expect to see a range of new offerings that cater to the diverse needs of investors. This chapter explores the potential future products and services that might emerge in the crypto ETF space.

1. Enhanced Crypto ETF Varieties

As the market matures, we can anticipate a broader variety of crypto ETFs that offer more refined investment strategies. This might include ETFs focusing on specific sub-sectors of the cryptocurrency market, such as DeFi (Decentralized Finance), NFTs (Non-Fungible Tokens), or specific blockchain protocols. Additionally, there could be more offerings of actively managed crypto ETFs, where fund managers actively select and trade digital assets rather than passively tracking an index.

2. Integration of Advanced Technologies

The integration of advanced technologies like AI (Artificial Intelligence) and ML (Machine Learning) in the management of crypto ETFs could become more prevalent. These technologies can enhance market analysis, trading strategies, and risk assessment, offering investors potentially higher returns and better risk management.

3. Customizable Crypto ETF Platforms

We may see the development of platforms that allow investors to customize their crypto ETFs. These platforms could enable investors to create personalized ETFs based on their chosen cryptocurrencies, risk profiles, and investment goals, similar to the concept of bespoke index funds.

4. Crypto ETFs with Built-in Tax Optimization

Given the complex tax implications of cryptocurrency investments, future crypto ETFs might come with built-in tax optimization strategies. These could include features like tax-loss harvesting and balancing between short-term and long-term gains to maximize tax efficiency.

5. Blockchain-Based ETF Trading Platforms

The use of blockchain technology in trading platforms for crypto ETFs could enhance transparency, security, and efficiency. Blockchain platforms can provide immutable transaction records, reduced counterparty risk, and potentially lower transaction costs.

6. ESG-Focused Crypto ETFs

As ESG (Environmental, Social, Governance) investing continues to gain traction, we might see the launch of ESG-focused crypto ETFs. These ETFs would invest in cryptocurrencies and blockchain companies that meet specific ESG criteria, appealing to socially conscious investors.

7. Derivative-Based Crypto ETFs

The introduction of derivative-based crypto ETFs, such as options and futures, could provide investors with tools for hedging and more sophisticated investment strategies. These ETFs would offer exposure to cryptocurrency markets through derivative instruments, potentially attracting a different class of investors.

8. Decentralized ETFs (dETFs)

The concept of decentralized ETFs, which operate on blockchain technology without a central managing authority, could emerge. These dETFs would leverage smart contracts for automated management, potentially reducing fees and democratizing access to investment products.

Conclusion

The potential for future products and services in the crypto ETF market is vast and exciting. From enhanced varieties of ETFs, integration of advanced technologies, and customizable platforms to ESG-focused products and innovative trading solutions, the landscape is ripe for innovation. These developments could significantly reshape the way investors interact with the cryptocurrency market, offering new opportunities for diversification, risk management, and growth. As the industry continues to evolve, staying informed and adaptable will be key for investors and financial advisors navigating this dynamic space.

Preparing for Technological Advancements in Crypto ETFs

As the worlds of finance and technology continue to converge, staying ahead in the rapidly evolving landscape of cryptocurrency ETFs requires preparation for imminent technological advancements. This chapter discusses strategies for investors and financial advisors to prepare for and leverage upcoming technological changes in the crypto ETF market.

1. Embracing Blockchain Innovations

Blockchain, the foundational technology behind cryptocurrencies, is continually advancing. Upcoming developments could include enhanced scalability, improved transaction speeds, and increased security features. Investors should stay informed about these advancements as they can significantly impact the performance and security of crypto ETFs.

2. Understanding Smart Contracts

Smart contracts are self-executing contracts with the terms of the agreement directly written into code. As they become more sophisticated, they could play a crucial role in automating and streamlining ETF transactions, reducing costs, and enhancing efficiency. A solid understanding of smart contracts will become increasingly important.

3. Keeping Abreast of Regulatory Technologies (RegTech)

Regulatory technologies aim to simplify compliance with financial regulations using technology. As crypto ETFs operate in a rapidly changing regulatory environment, being knowledgeable about RegTech can help investors and advisors navigate compliance more efficiently.

4. Exploring Decentralized Finance (DeFi) Platforms

DeFi platforms offer financial services using blockchain technology without traditional intermediaries. As these platforms grow, they could provide new ways to invest in or manage crypto ETFs. Familiarity with DeFi platforms and their potential integration with crypto ETFs is advisable.

5. Utilizing Advanced Analytics and AI

Artificial Intelligence (AI) and advanced analytics are becoming integral in financial markets for predicting market trends and optimizing investment strategies. Understanding how to utilize these tools for crypto ETF investments can provide a significant edge in portfolio management.

6. Leveraging Cryptocurrency Custody Solutions

As the market grows, the importance of secure cryptocurrency custody solutions becomes paramount. Investors should be aware of technological advancements in digital asset custody, such as multi-signature wallets and hardware security modules, to ensure the safekeeping of their investments.

7. Adapting to New Trading Platforms

Technological advancements may introduce new trading platforms or enhance existing ones for crypto ETFs. These platforms could offer improved user interfaces, better integration with other financial tools, and enhanced trading features.

8. Preparing for Quantum Computing

While still in the early stages, quantum computing presents a future challenge and opportunity. Its potential to break current encryption methods could impact cryptocurrency security, while also offering new solutions for complex financial modeling and data analysis. Staying informed about quantum computing developments is crucial.

9. Continuous Education and Adaptation

The key to preparing for technological advancements in crypto ETFs is continuous education and adaptability. Investors and advisors should engage in ongoing learning, attend industry conferences, participate in webinars, and subscribe to relevant publications.

Conclusion

Technological advancements in the crypto ETF market present both challenges and opportunities. By staying informed about blockchain innovations, smart contracts, RegTech, DeFi platforms, AI, custody solutions, and future developments like quantum computing, investors and advisors can position themselves to take advantage of these changes. Continuous education and a willingness to adapt are essential in navigating this dynamic and rapidly evolving landscape.

Conclusion 12. The Evolving Role of Financial Advisors

In the digital age, marked by rapid advancements in technology and a growing inclination towards cryptocurrencies and digital assets, the role of financial advisors is evolving significantly. No longer confined to traditional investment strategies, advisors are adapting to a landscape that now includes cryptocurrency ETFs, decentralized finance (DeFi), and blockchain technologies. This chapter explores how these changes are reshaping the responsibilities and skillsets of financial advisors.

The influx of digital assets into the market has necessitated a broader knowledge base. Advisors must now understand the complexities of blockchain technology, the intricacies of cryptocurrency markets, and the implications of digital assets on portfolio diversification and risk management. This shift demands continuous learning and adaptation to stay abreast of rapid market changes and technological advancements.

Moreover, the role of advisors is expanding to include educator and digital guide. Clients, ranging from tech-savvy millennials to traditional investors venturing into digital assets for the first time, seek advisors who can demystify the world of crypto investments and provide informed, strategic guidance. This role involves not only technical financial advising but also educating clients about the risks and potential rewards associated with these new asset classes.

Ethical and regulatory compliance has also become more complex. Advisors must navigate an evolving regulatory landscape, especially concerning cryptocurrencies and digital assets, ensuring that their advice remains compliant with current laws and ethical standards.

In conclusion, by embracing continuous education, technological proficiency, and adaptability, advisors can provide valuable guidance in this new era of finance, helping clients navigate a landscape that is at once exciting and challenging.

Adapting to a Changing Financial Landscape in the Era of Crypto ETFs

The financial landscape is undergoing a significant transformation, particularly with the advent of cryptocurrency ETFs (Exchange-Traded Funds). These changes necessitate a proactive and adaptive approach from investors and financial advisors. This chapter discusses strategies for adapting to the evolving financial environment, emphasizing the role of crypto ETFs.

1. Embracing Technological Advancements

The rapid pace of technological innovation is reshaping the financial sector. Blockchain technology, AI-driven analytics, decentralized finance (DeFi), and advanced cybersecurity measures are just a few examples. Staying abreast of these technologies and understanding how they impact investment products, particularly crypto ETFs, is crucial. Engaging with fintech developments can offer enhanced analysis, risk assessment, and investment opportunities.

2. Understanding the Evolving Nature of Cryptocurrencies

Cryptocurrencies, once a niche investment, have become more mainstream. However, they remain complex and often misunderstood. It is vital to understand the fundamentals of various cryptocurrencies, the technology behind them, their market dynamics, and their potential impact on the broader financial market. This knowledge is essential for effectively integrating crypto ETFs into investment portfolios.

3. Keeping Up with Regulatory Changes

The regulatory environment surrounding cryptocurrencies and crypto ETFs is still evolving. New regulations can significantly impact market dynamics and investment strategies. Staying informed about regulatory developments in different jurisdictions is essential for compliance and for anticipating market shifts that could affect investment decisions.

4. Revisiting Risk Management Strategies

The inclusion of crypto ETFs in investment portfolios introduces a different risk profile, marked by high volatility and unique market factors. It is important to revisit and adapt risk management strategies to accommodate these assets. This may involve adjusting portfolio diversification, setting stricter stop-loss orders, and regularly rebalancing portfolios to align with changing risk appetites.

5. Enhancing Client Communication and Education

As the financial landscape changes, so does the need for effective client communication and education. Clients may have varying levels of understanding and comfort with new financial products like crypto ETFs. Regular, transparent communication and educational efforts can help clients make informed decisions and feel more comfortable with their investment choices.

6. Fostering Flexibility in Investment Strategies

Flexibility is key in a changing financial landscape. This means being open to adjusting investment strategies, exploring new asset classes, and reconsidering traditional investment approaches. For instance, incorporating a mix of traditional and crypto ETFs or exploring thematic investments in emerging technologies can offer new growth opportunities.

7. Leveraging Professional Networks and Resources

Building and maintaining a strong professional network can provide valuable insights and resources. Joining industry forums, attending conferences, and participating in professional groups focused on cryptocurrencies and ETFs can offer the latest information and diverse perspectives.

8. Preparing for Market Volatility

Cryptocurrency markets are known for their volatility. Preparing for and navigating through these fluctuations requires a solid understanding of market triggers, effective use of hedging strategies, and maintaining a long-term investment perspective.

Conclusion

Adapting to the changing financial landscape in the era of crypto ETFs requires a multifaceted approach. It involves embracing technology, understanding the evolving nature of cryptocurrencies, staying informed about regulatory changes, revisiting risk management strategies, enhancing client communication, fostering investment flexibility, leveraging professional networks, and preparing for market volatility. By adopting these strategies, investors and advisors can navigate the dynamic financial environment effectively, capitalizing on new opportunities while managing the associated risks.

Embracing Innovation in Client Service in the Age of Crypto ETFs

In the rapidly evolving world of finance, especially with the introduction of cryptocurrency ETFs (Exchange-Traded Funds), embracing innovation in client service has become crucial. This chapter explores how financial advisors and investment firms can enhance client service by integrating innovative practices, particularly in the context of the emerging crypto ETF market.

1. Leveraging Digital Platforms for Enhanced Communication

The digital revolution offers an array of tools for improving client communication. Advisors can utilize various platforms such as secure messaging apps, video conferencing, and client portals to provide timely updates, market insights, and personalized advice. These tools can foster more frequent and efficient interactions, keeping clients informed and engaged.

2. Offering Educational Resources on Cryptocurrency and Blockchain

Given the complexities and novelty of crypto ETFs, providing clients with comprehensive educational resources is essential. This can include webinars, detailed guides, and interactive workshops that cover the basics of cryptocurrencies, blockchain technology, and the specifics of crypto ETFs. Education empowers clients to make more informed investment decisions.

3. Utilizing AI and Machine Learning for Customized Investment Insights

Artificial Intelligence (AI) and Machine Learning (ML) can analyze vast amounts of data to derive insights that might be invisible to the human eye. By leveraging these technologies, advisors can offer highly personalized investment advice, tailor portfolio recommendations, and provide predictive market analysis, enhancing the overall quality of client service.

4. Implementing Advanced Analytics for Portfolio Management

Advanced analytics tools can provide a deeper understanding of portfolio performance, risk factors, and market trends. These tools can help advisors in delivering a more sophisticated analysis to clients, explaining the impact of various assets, including crypto ETFs, on their investment goals.

5. Fostering Transparency Through Blockchain Technology

Blockchain technology can be used to enhance transparency in client transactions and portfolio management. Implementing blockchain-based systems can provide clients with real-time, tamper-proof records of their investments, fostering trust and transparency in client relationships.

6. Personalizing Client Experiences with Robo-Advisory Services

Robo-advisors, powered by algorithms, can offer personalized investment advice and automated portfolio management. They can complement traditional advisory services, providing clients with a more diverse range of options to manage their investments, including crypto ETFs.

7. Embracing Mobile Solutions for On-the-Go Access

Mobile applications allow clients to access their investment information, market updates, and advisory services anytime and anywhere. Developing or leveraging robust mobile platforms can significantly enhance client experience, offering convenience and immediate access to crucial information.

8. Staying Ahead of Regulatory Changes and Compliance

In the fast-changing regulatory landscape of cryptocurrencies, advisors need to stay informed about compliance and regulatory requirements. Offering clients guidance on these aspects, especially in relation to crypto ETFs, is part of innovative client service.

Conclusion

Embracing innovation in client service is vital in the age of crypto ETFs and digital finance. By leveraging digital communication tools, providing educational resources, utilizing AI and advanced analytics, ensuring transparency, personalizing experiences, and staying informed about regulatory changes, financial advisors and firms can offer superior service. This approach not only enhances client engagement and trust but also positions advisors as leaders in the dynamic and evolving world of investment management.

Future Outlook for Financial Advisors with Crypto Expertise

In the contemporary landscape of finance, the burgeoning relevance of cryptocurrencies and related investment vehicles like crypto ETFs (Exchange-Traded Funds) is reshaping the role and skills required of financial advisors. This chapter examines the future outlook for financial advisors who specialize in or possess substantial expertise in cryptocurrencies and blockchain technology.

1. Growing Demand for Crypto-Savvy Advisors

As cryptocurrencies gain mainstream acceptance and become a more integral part of investment portfolios, the demand for financial advisors with crypto expertise is expected to grow. Investors, ranging from individuals to large institutions, are seeking advisors who not only understand traditional investment vehicles but are also adept at navigating the complex and rapidly evolving world of digital assets.

2. Enhanced Service Offering and Competitive Edge

Financial advisors with a deep understanding of crypto assets can offer a broader range of services to their clients. This expertise not only includes investment advice related to crypto ETFs but also extends to areas like tax implications of crypto investments, regulatory compliance, and blockchain technology's impact on various sectors. Advisors with these skills will likely have a competitive edge in an industry that increasingly values technological proficiency and innovative investment strategies.

3. Diversification of Advisory Practices

The rise of cryptocurrencies is encouraging financial advisors to diversify their practices. Advisors can expand their services to include crypto portfolio management, blockchain consulting, and educational workshops on digital assets. This diversification not only enhances the advisor's value proposition but also helps in attracting a wider range of clients, including younger, tech-savvy investors.

4. Increased Collaboration with Tech Experts and Regulators

The future will likely see increased collaboration between financial advisors, technology experts, and regulatory bodies. As crypto markets continue to mature, advisors will need to stay abreast of technological advancements, regulatory changes, and compliance requirements. Establishing strong networks with tech experts and regulatory authorities will be crucial.

5. Emphasis on Continuing Education and Professional Development

To remain relevant and effective, financial advisors with crypto expertise will need to commit to continuous learning and professional development. The field of cryptocurrency is characterized by rapid changes and requires advisors to stay informed about the latest market developments, technological innovations, and investment products.

6. Navigating Ethical and Compliance Challenges

As with any emerging asset class, cryptocurrencies bring unique ethical and compliance challenges. Advisors will need to navigate these challenges carefully, ensuring that they maintain high ethical standards and adhere strictly to evolving regulatory requirements, particularly in areas like anti-money laundering (AML) and know your customer (KYC) regulations.

7. Leveraging Technology for Client Engagement and Advisory

Advisors specializing in cryptocurrencies will increasingly leverage technology for client engagement and advisory services. This includes utilizing digital platforms for client communication, employing advanced analytics for investment analysis, and adopting blockchain-based tools for portfolio management.

Conclusion

The future outlook for financial advisors with expertise in cryptocurrencies and blockchain technology is highly promising. As the demand for knowledge and skills in this area grows, advisors who equip themselves with crypto expertise and a keen understanding of the associated technological and regulatory nuances are well-positioned for success. They will play a pivotal role in guiding investors through the intricacies of digital asset investments, helping to shape a future where traditional and innovative investment strategies coexist and complement each other.

Appendices

Glossary of Terms

1. **Blockchain**: A distributed ledger technology that maintains a decentralized and secure record of transactions across a network of computers.
2. **Cryptocurrency**: Digital or virtual currencies that use cryptography for security, operating independently of a central bank.
3. **Crypto ETF (Cryptocurrency Exchange-Traded Fund)**: An investment fund traded on stock exchanges that tracks the performance of one or several cryptocurrencies.
4. **DeFi (Decentralized Finance)**: Financial services built on blockchain technologies that operate without traditional centralized intermediaries.
5. **Digital Asset**: A digital representation of value or contractual rights that can be transferred and stored electronically.
6. **ETF (Exchange-Traded Fund)**: A type of security that tracks an index, commodity, sector, or other assets, but can be bought and sold like a stock on a stock exchange.
7. **Futures Contract**: A financial contract obligating the buyer to purchase an asset or the seller to sell an asset at a predetermined future date and price.
8. **Liquidity**: The ability to quickly buy or sell an asset without causing a significant price change.

9. **Market Volatility**: The rate at which the price of an investment increases or decreases for a given set of returns.

10. **NFT (Non-Fungible Token)**: A unique digital identifier that cannot be copied, substituted, or subdivided, recorded in a blockchain, and used to certify authenticity and ownership.

11. **Portfolio Diversification**: An investment strategy that spreads risk by allocating investments among various financial instruments, industries, and other categories.

12. **RegTech (Regulatory Technology)**: The management of regulatory processes within the financial industry through technology.

13. **Risk Tolerance**: An investor's ability or willingness to endure declines in the values of investments.

14. **Smart Contract**: A self-executing contract with the terms of the agreement between buyer and seller directly written into lines of code.

15. **Tax-Loss Harvesting**: An investment strategy that involves selling securities at a loss to offset a capital gains tax liability.

16. **Trading Volume**: The amount of an asset or security that trades hands over a specific period.

17. **Traditional Assets**: Conventional investment assets like stocks, bonds, and cash.

18. **Transactional Security**: Measures taken to ensure the security and integrity of financial transactions, particularly in digital formats.

19. **Wealth Management**: Professional services that combine financial and investment advice, accounting and tax services, retirement planning, and legal or estate planning for one fee.

This glossary provides key terms that will help readers navigate the complex world of cryptocurrency investments and ETFs, enhancing their understanding of the material covered in "Crypto ETFs in the Financial Advisor's Toolkit: Enhancing Client Wealth."

Useful Resources for Financial Advisors

Check out other titles in the Crypto Wisdom Series (**CryptoWisdom.com**):

- *Crypto Wisdom: An Investor's Comprehensive Guide to Digital Asset Research and Analysis: A Step-by-Step Guide to Researching and Analyzing Digital Assets for Building Winning Portfolios*

- *Crypto Wisdom: An Investor's Comprehensive Guide to Digital Asset Portfolio Management: A Step-by-Step Guide for Building Winning Crypto Portfolios*

- *The Financial Advisor's Digital Asset Practice Guide: A Step-by-Step Guide to Building a Digital Asset Practice*

- *The Investment Advisor's Cryptocurrency Roadmap: The Guide to Offering Cryptocurrencies and Digital Assets in Your Practice*

- *Mastering the Crypto ETF Wave: A Comprehensive Guide to Researching and Investing*

- *Crypto Bites: Snack-sized insights for the Modern Investor*

Smart Kids Series (Teaching kids of all ages about bitcoin, blockchain and more)

- *Bitcoin Smart Kids: Teaching Kids of Every Age About Bitcoin*

- *Blockchain Smart Kids: Teaching Kids of Every Age How Blockchain and Bitcoin Work Together*

- *Metaverse Smart Kids: Teaching Kids of Every Age About the Metaverse*

Visit **www.CryptoWisdom.com** for complete step-by-step training, cryptocurrency educational videos, etc.